Singled Out
For God's
Assignment

A Widow's Valley of
Learning

Singled Out For God's Assignment

A Widow's Valley of Learning

Leona Choy

Golden Morning Publishing
Winchester, Virginia

Singled Out for God's Assignment: *A Widow's Valley of Learning*
© 1996 Leona Choy

Published by *Golden Morning Publishing*
P.O. Box 2697, Winchester, VA 22604

Cover photography by B.J. Roderick

Library of Congress Cataloging-in-Publication Data

Choy, Leona
    Singled Out For God's Assignment: A Widow's Valley of Learning

ISBN 1-889283-03-7
    1. Non-fiction—Religion—Christianity—Grieving

Published in the United States of America

Printed in the USA by

MORRIS PUBLISHING

3212 E. Hwy 30
Kearney, NE 68847
800-650-7888

Books by Leona Choy

Authored, edited or collaborated,
including foreign language editions

A Call To The Church From Wang Mingdao
Andrew Murray, Apostle Of Abiding Love.
      Spanish, Dutch, Chinese, Afrikaans, Korean editions
Christiana Tsai. Also Chinese edition
Divine Applications (poetry)
Heart Cry Of China. Also Chinese edition
His Mighty Power/Esther Wang
Heaven and Nature Sing (poetry)
The Holy Spirit and His Work/A.B.Simpson
Hospital Gowns Don't Have Pockets:
      Discovering Meaning in Physical Distress
How to Capture and Develop Ideas for Writing
Improving Our Cross-cultural Postures:Missions on the Level
The Inner Chamber/Andrew Murray (Contemporized)
Jewels From The Queen Of The Dark Chamber/
      Christiana Tsai. Also in Chinese.
The Key To The Missionary Problem/Andrew Murray
      (Contemporized). Nigerian and Portuguese editions
Life—Stop Crowding Me! (poetry)
Let My People Go!/Moses C.Chow with Leona Choy
No Ground/Evelyn Carter Spencer with Leona Choy
On Your Mark: A Christian Traveler's Guide to China
Powerlines. Also Chinese and Korean editions
Release the Poet Within!
      How to Launch and Improve Poetry Craft and Ministry
Singled Out for God's Assignment: A Widow's Valley of Learning
Songs of My Pilgrimage (poetry)
The State Of The Church/Andrew Murray (Contemporized)
Touching China: Close Encounters of the Christian Kind
The Widow's Might: Strength from the ROCK

About the Author

Born of Czech parents in Iowa and a graduate of Wheaton College, Illinois, Leona Choy served with her late husband, Ted, in mission, church and educational work in Hong Kong, Singapore, China and the United States. Co-founder of *Ambassadors For Christ, Inc.*, a campus ministry for Chinese university students and scholars, her quarter century of work was administrative and editorial.

Fourteen trips to the People's Republic of China as guide/escort and English teaching consultant enriched her research and experiences for writing. As President of *WTRM-FM (Southern Light Gospel Music Network)* in the Shenandoah Valley of Virginia, Leona produced a daily radio program for five years.

Author, editor or collaborator of over 25 published books and 12 foreign language editions, her articles have appeared in over 70 different periodicals. Leona's poems have been published in scores of magazines and read over her daily radio programs, *Intensive Care,* and *Living It Up* on *WTRM.*

She is managing editor of *Golden Morning Publishing* in Winchester, Virginia, where she makes her home. Four grown sons and seven grandchildren keep her busy when she isn't writing or traveling.

Dedication

To all friends
who share my
"singled out" status
by God's appointment.

Preface

On the second anniversary of Ted's death, I rummaged in the storage area for a slab of birch wood with an oil painting of a sea gull winging off into the sky—alone. Our son, Clifford, bought it for me while he vacationed at the beach some years before. I hung it in my dining area. For me it symbolized finally moving on, soaring into the unknown as a single again—but with God.

As a new widow, I had set a higher standard than God did by trying to hurry toward adjustment. That proved premature. I needed to take my time and cross a *natural bridge* over my troubled waters. *That bridge was the healthy grieving process* which God lovingly provides for those who lose someone they love. Because I tried to skip it I fell into foaming rapids of unresolved emotions, bruising myself on rocks hidden by the spray.

Better late than never, I realized my need to confront and embrace my honest emotions. I had to go back and cross that bridge before I could move on to healthy personhood as a single and experience the delight of finding God's new assignment.

Then my Valley of Grief became a joyful Valley of Learning!

Leona Choy

Foreword

If the widows I counseled had read Leona's book soon after the death of their husbands, many may not have needed my services. I read Leona's manuscript from cover to cover. As a practicing psychiatrist for many years, I would have eagerly recommended her book to my patients had it been available. Especially to "singled out" widows who were Bible-believing Christians.

Grief has touched all of creation ever since Adam and Eve "blew it" (sinned) by disobeying God in Eden's garden. It can occur after any profound loss—possessions, security, health, abilities, job—even pets. But most intensely after the loss of significant persons.

I have treated widows, of whom there are five times as many as widowers, suffering from clinical depression, including physical symptoms. Many are unable to adjust to their new roles alone and have difficulty functioning in daily life. Others cannot see themselves as having any meaningful future. Some require medication in addition to psychotherapy.

But certainly not all grieving requires intervention by a professional. That's where Leona's book comes in. She addresses a wide variety of facets arising from widowhood, especially for women who are Christ-ones. It's difficult to imagine any she has overlooked. She probes the subject from multiple directions, enriching the text with valuable resource quotations. Almost like a roving reporter at a baseball game, she "interviews" singled out friends and shares case histories, while basing her observations squarely on the Scriptures.

Leona blends her biblical knowledge with an intimate understanding of the emotions experienced almost universally after the death of a spouse. She writes from the vantage point of having weathered them—but not without struggles—in the years following the death of her husband, Ted. Leona allows herself to be vulnerable, admitting mistakes she made as she attempted to skip parts of the grieving process because they didn't seem "Christian" to her. The reader can readily identify with her.

This book deserves a broad and lengthy circulation. Its use may well decrease both the depth and duration of the grieving process and diminish the need for professional intervention. Putting the principles and concepts into practice could hasten adjustment and provide direction for a fresh walk with God in a meaningful new role.

Widows and widowers are not the only ones who may benefit from this book. Families and friends of the bereaved, pastors, counselors and caregivers may read it with profit to understand the grieving process and help the hurting through it.

I have known the author for many years to be honest, direct and perceptively sensitive. Leona's writing makes sense to me professionally as well as personally. If one reading doesn't suffice to plumb its depths for you—try another walk through it.

Chester L. Schneider, M.D.
Former medical missionary and
retired clinical psychiatrist.

Contents

I have come to understand that even suffering, through the transforming power of the Cross, is a gift, for in this broken world, in our sorrow, He gives us Himself; in our loneliness He comes to meet us. . . .

The Lord who had given me singleness and marriage as gifts of His love, had now given me this new gift of widowhood. [1]

Elisabeth Elliot

1 *Singled Out by God*

ou may be newly widowed, or already alone for many years. Wherever you are on your adjustment journey without your spouse, may we agree on something? As a *Christian* widow, you have been *singled out, deliberately chosen, selected* by our loving God for your present role. You have not been derailed from God's plan for your life when your marriage ended. Your influence and witness are not over. God has a continuing agenda for you.

Throughout this book I use the term *singled out* to describe us. Not *widow*, but "singled out" in the sense of being *appointed* by God for our new status.

Another way of looking at our unasked-for but appointed singleness is to consider it a gift from God. In the throes of our early bereavement we want to refuse that gift. Isn't a gift supposed to be something wonderful, something desired? We certainly didn't want to be widows!

Some of us are even angry with God. The death of our life companion doesn't seem like God's loving gift. Some of us try to hold our hands over our ears and don't even want to hear Scriptural words of comfort. The Lord is gentle, full of compassion and patient. He tenderly sees us through our initial grief and shepherds us into His plans for our future.

Elisabeth Elliot, noted author and missionary, whose first husband, Jim, was murdered by the Auca Indians, tells of her delight with God's gifts of marriage and motherhood after many years of waiting.

Suddenly . . .

I was not a wife anymore. I was a widow. Another assignment. Another "gift." I began to see that there is a sense in which everything is a gift, even my widowhood. . . . [God] had done more than merely "allow" a thing to "happen" *to* me. I do not know any more accurate way of putting it than to say that He had given me . . . a *gift*—widowhood. How can I say such a thing?

I've come to understand that even suffering, through the transforming power of the Cross, is a *gift*, for in this broken world, *in* our sorrow, He gives us Himself; *in* our loneliness He comes to meet us. . . .

The Lord, who had given me singleness and marriage as gifts of His love, had now given me this one. Would I receive it from His hand? Would I thank Him for it? [1]

Although it was difficult, Elisabeth accepted her gift, thanked God for it and reached out for her new assignment.

Your spouse has gone on ahead, but your Lord has *further marching orders* for you, too. Perhaps renewed marching orders in the same direction, or different in *some* respects—or *totally* different. Whatever God's assignment, you will no longer carry it out as a married couple. Nevertheless, you *will* carry it out as a *couple!*

There will still be *two*—*God and you!*

As Christian women we know in our heads and our hearts that we don't live in a random universe. Things don't happen haphazardly to God's children. Everything is under His control, has ultimate meaning and is timed for His glory and our good. God is good and does all things well. Romans 8:28 and 29 apply to us—all things *do* work together for good to those who love God.

Still, our pain seems so deep and personal. When death comes to someone close to us, we tend to lose perspective. We're overcome with grief as if we were the first ones to experience it.

The fact is, three-fourths of American wives will someday become widows. I'm not alone, but I feel alone because it is *my* grief.

Most of us put our heads in the sand and pretend that we will live "happily ever after" on earth. We plan for every other stage of life and enthusiastically read how-to-do-it books about everything—except death. We go through premarital counseling and expectant parents classes, but no one offers a widowhood seminar for married women to prepare for such a major and probable life event.

We don't want to face the fact that everyone who lives on planet earth dies. The loss of my husband is not some strange and unusual occurrence. Death is inevitable. It came to my husband first, but it could just as easily have left him a widower. Death will eventually come to me. Our times are in God's hands.

However, joy is over the horizon! I suggest that being a widow is only a transition period. Widowhood is not like a disease, terminal illness or accident. Since God is unquestionably trustworthy, He guarantees that we will recover. We don't need to think of ourselves as widows for the rest of our lives. Not because we may marry again, although we may, but because widowhood is a temporary period to *pass through* as we move toward normal, healthy, *single personhood.*

Calling ourselves widows symbolizes a continuing connection to our marriage, but death ended that tie. However wonderful our marriage may have been, it is now in the past. Widowhood isn't a *rut* to get stuck in forever, or a no-exit *cave* in which to settle. It is a *tunnel* with an *exit.*

The Lord, our Light, wants to lead us through this tunnel of widowhood *not somehow, but triumphantly!* As we make our way through, we will gradually begin to understand the assignment He has for us. Let's trust God to see us through *together.* You are not alone. I'll hold your hand, and the Lord will hold *our* hands.

Not Alone

As I enter the tunnel
of an unfamiliar experience
I feel desperately alone.
Darkness shrouds me
I grope around
trying to manage on my own.

Then, as I reach out,
I touch someone's hand:
it warmly grasps mine

speaking volumes
an understanding squeeze
without words
reassuring me
that I'm not alone!

Another fearful hand
reaches out for mine
so I offer
the same encouraging grip
that I've received.
We're bound together now
in a common journey
a mutual quest.

Relieved of our isolated fear
comforted by someone near
we make our way together
friend with friend
through the unfamiliar tunnel
toward the open end.

Suddenly our way is illumined
by the radiant presence
of The Greatest Friend
Who said, "I am the Light"
and *we're truly*
no longer alone.
We emerge together
triumphantly! [2]

Almost immediately after my husband's death I
had to fill out some forms which gave me only two choices:
"married" or "single." No little square to check "other."

My hand shook as I checked "single" for the very first time. Then I decided to qualify it by putting (widow) in parentheses.

The "single" and "widow" categories were new and unfamiliar. Only the day before, I would have checked "married." The dictionary defines a widow as "a woman whose husband has died and who has not remarried."

"Widow" does define me, as much as I'd like to avoid that label. I join literally millions in that category.

I'm also *single again.*

I was married for 45 years, more than twice as long as I was single the first time.

When Ted and I married, two singles became one flesh. While we were married, we were united as a couple, although remaining two distinct people. Now, separated by death, I'm a single person again.

"Single" does describe me, as much as I'd like to avoid that name tag, too. I join literally millions of women and men in that category.

During the first year after Ted's death I journaled my feelings, fears, victories, failures and struggles. On this journey I alternately experienced shadowy valleys and sunny mountain tops. At times I dragged my feet over plateaus that seemed like endless deserts. It was right at the beginning that I made a major mistake— what I thought was a victorious response to my loss was actually an unnatural one.

> [Delaying grief work] is the most common abnormal grief response. The manifestation of this response is usually calm, even magnificent acceptance of the tragedy. At the funeral home [the widow] quotes the right Scriptures and actually comforts those who came to comfort her. But months later, when

everyone else has gotten on with their lives, she falls apart.[3]

Whoa! Could that describe *me?* I confess that *was* my experience. I didn't intend to take the wrong road. I wanted to cruise right in the middle of God's highway and follow His will completely. No one intends to get lost or take the wrong fork at a crossroad.

One night I was driving some friends to a writers' meeting an hour's distance from home. After a while the road began to look unfamiliar and scary.

"Somehow I must have missed the right road," I confessed. "I'll have to go back."

Embarrassed, I turned the car around in a dark driveway and retraced my route until I found where I had made my error. I sincerely thought I knew the right road, but my sincerity didn't avert my time-consuming mistake. Returning to where I made the error and proceeding in the right direction was critical.

Two years after the death of my husband I thought this book was ready for publication. Having journaled my personal widowhood experience, I thought it would be helpful to other Christian women. However, through a series of God-appointed circumstances, months of serious attention to the experiences of others who lost spouses, listening to friends who were professional grief counselors, and attending a workshop on emotional resolution given by a colleague—I was stopped short.

Instead of being ready to publish, I discovered with a shock that the book I had been writing to help other widows recorded *an incomplete experience.* I had described "part two," the *latter* part of the loss journey— moving on toward adjustment and new assignment. I had not internalized and worked through "part one," the essential, foundational grieving process that leads to healing and adjustment in a more natural way.

I almost expected God to reprimand me if I didn't rejoice immediately at my husband's promotion to heaven. However, rejoicing and healing usually come gradually as God's comfort seeps through to the core of one's being.

Somehow I missed a whole important section of the recovery road. The later stages of my adjustment and healing would have been flawed had I not retraced my steps. I made a personal U - turn and began to grapple with and work through some of the universal feelings of the grieving process I had neglected and downplayed.

Had I not done so, (even two years later!) and painfully struggled through the stretch of experience I missed, I could have misled some who would pick up this book expecting realistic, sensitive help for their own loss-journey. I might have led them astray by my incomplete example. They might have tried reaching for their new assignment *before* paying their dues by going through a normal, good grieving process.

I had never been a widow before. I was sincere in assuming that a Christian should grab a vine, as Tarzan did, and *swing over* the chasm between loss and moving on. I tried to act the part of "superlady" because I thought my family and friends expected me to.

I had to learn that a widow's journey is not an airborne experience by which she can fly over the inevitable, prescribed landscape of loss. I can't take a helicopter over grieving just because I have strong Christian faith, trust in God's sovereignty and am sure that my husband is safe and happy in the presence of Jesus. Yes, "underneath are the everlasting arms," and we are uniquely sheltered by the Lord during initial shock. Christians do have the wonderful, eternal hope that Paul wrote about, contrasted in First Thessalonians with "those who have no hope."

Nevertheless, we can't hop in a plane called "Hope" and rise above normal, human feelings. Good grieving is a *ground transportation* experience.

Sometimes we must make our way over rough terrain, struggling uphill, sometimes coasting back downhill. At times we end in ditches at the side of the road.

To grieve or not to grieve? I honestly thought that was the question—and my quick answer was—*I am not supposed to grieve.* One reason I was reluctant to permit myself to grieve normally was because I assumed grieving meant only tearful mourning and emotional carrying on for the loved one who died. Such grieving seemed incompatible not only with my Christian faith but that of my minister/missionary husband, Ted. He preached and lived with strong faith in eternal life and joyfully anticipated Heaven. Should I now grieve for his supreme happiness?

I missed the point again—I defined grieving too narrowly. I've come to realize that grieving is not limited to sorrow *for* the person who has departed or necessarily demonstrated by tears. Each of us is different so each must find her own way in her own time. The outward expression of grieving varies according to our personalities, our experiences, relationships, circumstances, even cultural backgrounds. An initial, limited period of natural grieving can and should be creative and lead to recovery. God intends for us to emerge as stronger, whole women and better equipped to help others.

Nor is grieving simply a matter of self-pity. It has wider facets that we will explore together. It is to be embraced, not avoided.

Grief is not a sign of weakness. It is, rather, a healthy and fitting response to a loss, a tribute to a loved one who has died. Running away from grief prolongs sorrow; clinging to grief prolongs pain. Neither approach leads to healing. Allow grief to have its way for a while; then, gradually and gently, you can release yourself from its grip. Recognition of the appropriateness and value of grief is the first step in accepting the reality of the loss. And acceptance is the first sign of recovery. [4]

I had to learn the hard way—in the early months I shouldn't have run away from grieving or tried so hard to keep my emotions always under control. I should have said to grief: *Hello. I didn't invite you, but I believe God sent you to be my teacher. Since you've come, sit with me awhile. I know you won't stay forever. You'll move on and so will I. I will listen and learn from you.*

This is a sharing book, not a how-to-do-it handbook. Space doesn't allow me to cover all the different aspects of widowhood, address the specific adjustments of young widows who still have small children to raise, or speak to widows whose husbands were not Christians. Or widowers who face some unique problems in everyday living and emotional adjustments. My heart goes out to all of you. I have written specifically for the Christian widow who has lost her Christian husband.

However, many principles, experiences and suggestions are applicable to all the above categories of grievers. I welcome you, no matter what your circumstances of loss, to help yourself to transferable concepts from which you might benefit. Together let's learn about normally processing healthy grief, gently closing the door on our past, eagerly opening new doors God has set before us, and moving courageously forward to find our assignment from Him. 🌺

Some Christians have mistakenly thought that grief demonstrates a lack of faith. Thus they have felt it necessary to maintain strength rather than deal honestly with a painful loss. Good grief is grief that enables us to make the transition to a new phase of existence. The widow must learn to live alone. . . . Grief that deals honestly with the pain is a part of the healing process.[1]

Erwin W. Lutzer

Experiencing "Good Grief"

 $\mathcal{A}$s a newly singled out Christian woman I wrestled with basic questions:

🌱 What is grieving? Is it mainly tearful crying?

🌱 If I don't express grief outwardly, do I not grieve?

🌱 Can I control grief—to either express or suppress it?

🌱 If I suppress it, is it always unhealthy and unwise?

🌱 Does grief involve other emotions? Hurt? Memories? Regrets? Forgiveness?

🌱 Is grieving something I do or something I feel?

🌱 What does "process my grief" mean?

🌱 How does my grief as a Christian differ from that of a non-Christian?

The answers to some of those questions are deeply personal and differ from one individual to another. Some answers are in a "gray area." Each of us needs to identify her own temperament and personal needs and permit God's gentle Spirit to do His perfect work while she walks through her valley with Him.

Some people are by nature not demonstrative, nevertheless they work through the process inwardly in their own way. The last thing such people need is someone pushing them to express their grief outwardly. Let's be sensitive to individual grieving patterns and be available to one another, encouraging but not judgmental, if we don't express grief in the same way.

Christian distinctives

The apostle Paul taught that we shouldn't "grieve like those who have no hope." His instruction affirms the reality of grief among all people, but implies that the Christian's grief should be distinctive. I believe Paul was pointing out that we should acknowledge grief, not set aside our emotions, but express grief distinctively because of our Christian faith. First-century pagans viewed death with horror and carried on wild, emotional demonstrations of grief (sometimes hiring professional mourners to weep and wail) because they considered death the end of everything. The Christian outlook stands in strong contrast.

Tears and sorrow are normal but the difference is between tears of hope and tears of hopelessness. The nonbeliever's grief is *truly* hopeless—literally a dead-end, a termination, and does result in intense emotional suffering. They see no light at the end of their tunnel. That's why the Bible compassionately, not judgmentally, refers to such people as *"those who have no hope."*

However, Christians do have a hope. Not in the sense of the wistful little boy who said, "Hope is wishing hard for something you know you're not going to get." Our hope is the assurance that "everything is going to turn out just like our good God intended it!" Jesus declared, "I am the resurrection and the life; he who believes in Me shall live even if he dies, and everyone who lives and believes in Me shall never die. Do you believe this?" (John 11:25,26). That's the Christian's hope. Yes, I believe that. Paul declared that death lost its sting because Christ was victorious over it. "Therefore . . . stand firm. Let nothing move you. . . ." (1 Corinthians 15:53-58).

While mysteries remain, 2 Corinthians 5:6-10 clearly teaches that when believers die they are immediately with Christ, separated from their bodies. Paul claimed, "to depart and be with Christ is . . . better by far" (Philippians 1:23). As a Christian, I accept the truth that my Christian husband is in that far-better place. He is beyond pain and suffering. He's not in limbo or some kind of unconscious state. He is consciously enjoying incredible delights and wonders and the expansion of his knowledge and powers in an immortal state. He recognizes fellow saints through the ages and is celebrating his new freedom. It is fitting not to grieve *for him*.

I initially misunderstood that if I expressed grief, I would be disobedient to Scriptural truth. What I didn't understand is the grieving process as experienced by a Christian.

Human grief *is* a valid feeling, normal *and not unspiritual.* Human emotional attachments are strong—they can't be quickly dismissed.

I frankly needed time to grieve for what my husband and I would never do together again, for the sadness of his unfulfilled plans to keep traveling in missions ministry and for his anticipation of spending more time with his family now that he had retired. I needed to grieve for small things like his overgrown garden, the ripe fruit unpicked on tall, productive trees he planted as young saplings, for not being able to attend his family reunion for which he was packed to leave when he died. For missing the joy of knowing he was to have a new grandchild. Not to know what our sons would be doing in their careers. What new books were on the horizon for me. I would miss his valuable participation in research and critique.

I needed to give myself permission to grieve when I recalled my activities that morning before I knew my husband had already arrived in the presence of the Lord. I arose early to greet a frosty, clear morning. Sunshine flooded the kitchen as I cooked oatmeal which I knew Ted would appreciate on a cold morning. I ate a bowlful and left his portion with a note to remind him where I was going. I assumed he was having an extended quiet time of prayer and Bible reading, his lifelong habit, so I didn't disturb him. I drove off for an early medical appointment.

Afterward I stopped at the floor covering shop to take another look at the carpeting we had nearly decided on for the chalet we were building. Arriving home, I was surprised that he hadn't eaten breakfast yet, but I spent 15 minutes at the computer editing notes he had written on the history of our mission.

Suddenly I felt an urgency to go upstairs and see if he had finished packing for his trip to California the next day. He didn't answer my knock. I opened the door to find him still lying peacefully in bed, blankets undisturbed. The Lord had taken him "home" during the night.

I can hardly remember what happened the rest of that day.

Grief deprivation

I saw a documentary on TV about the effects of sleep deprivation. Too little sleep results in certain dangerous symptoms. Too much sleep conversely disturbs the delicate balance of need. Each of us has his own body clock to let him know when enough is enough or too much.

We can also suffer from *grief deprivation*. I did, and wasn't aware of it, although others have since told me they suspected it. When I denied my need for grief, it was as foolish as denying my need for sleep. Do I consider it a waste of time to spend seven or eight hours every night sleeping and doing nothing productive? Especially when life at best is so short? That adds up to 56 "useless" hours a week—nearly 3,000 hours a year! Surely that isn't "redeeming the time" as the Bible instructs.

Of course that is absurd reasoning. I guess I used the same absurd logic to conclude that if I spent weeks or months in a grieving process, I would be a poor steward of my time and disappoint my Lord.

I was wrong. Grief deprivation has inevitable consequences. If I skipped it early in the process, I would eventually have to do remedial work. If I didn't, I couldn't move on in a healthy, balanced direction. My adjustment would be incomplete.

My flawed game plan had been to anesthetize my grief and prematurely give birth to an adjusted life and a new assignment without undue personal pain.

In hindsight, I see that my sincere strategy was unnatural. Current obstetric practice favors natural childbirth, if possible, with the mother's conscious cooperation, working through real pain to a more healthy delivery. In a similar way, to cooperatively, consciously work through grief is God's natural process.

But how long?

Grieving is not a permanent state. It is only for a season, usually the initial season, unless the process gets sidetracked like mine did. Calling it a season implies that it will give way in time to another temporary season—there is a duration and an end. We can't put a definite date on a season's closure in nature. The calendar suggests when winter is supposed to be over and spring should begin, but weather often doesn't cooperate with the calendar. In a similar way, God has a timetable for my grieving process. It may be longer or shorter than the one He has for someone else. The grieving process lasts for however long a particular woman needs to achieve emotional and spiritual stability and health. Nevertheless, I make a mistake if I try to deny the need for it or avoid it.

We should not be in a hurry. The length of time needed to work through grief *may or may not* depend on how long a couple was married, their age, circumstances of death, or their degree of dependence on each other. Personal temperament, past role models of grieving, the influence of church and culture all play a part, and whether she has supportive relationships and meaningful prospects for the future.

Be patient then. Give yourself a chance to learn how to live without the other. Why get busy so soon? Running. . .running. . .running . . . Why pretend that we don't have difficult feelings? Is it because we're ingrained with the American Dream, the Good Life? To be strong? Not to show feelings? To have it all together?

Can you afford one year, a few months, or a couple of weeks to adjust? One year to learn to change a relationship of 30 years? Give yourself a chance. Don't try to pull out so fast! Be patient. Take some time. Learn to live again. Altering love ties is difficult and painful work; it does not come easily or quickly.

Part of you is gone—that's why you feel loss. The feeling that is not expressed is left screaming for expression. So face feeling.[2]

Evaluating the advice of comforters

Job, whose struggles, the Bible recounts, had some of his greatest frustrations with his friends. Poor Job. With friends like his, who needs enemies? They were well-meaning, but largely off-base in their counsel. Those of us trying to make our way through the grieving process need wisdom and sometimes a heavy dose of restraint when friends give us inappropriate advice. We are the only ones who can know what is best for us, under the counsel of the Lord.

My friend Sally, singled out about the same time I was, wrote of her experience:

I have to keep reminding myself to trust the Lord and not accept all the advice given by

well-wishers who pass it out so freely. They
have never walked in my shoes. They strongly
advised me that I must have a co-worker to
take Larry's place in our missionary ministry,
but the Lord impressed me clearly that I should
quietly continue working alone. This proved to
be the best course.

I have kind friends who phone and say
they are praying hard that someone will move
in with me in my small house. My whole being
cries *no!* Yes, I get lonesome at times, but this
was the house Larry and I shared for so many
years. I miss him desperately, but without
anyone here I can go to bed and get up when I
choose, leave the TV off, stay up and read if I
choose, prepare what I want to eat, and have
my quiet time alone.

My house is big enough for me and very
comfortable. To move a stranger in I'd have to
get rid of so many of our personal things. I
simply want to live alone. My friends shake
their heads and think I'm resisting what is best
for me.

With good intentions they tried to load
me with jobs, even assigned me to call on shut-
ins immediately after Larry died. But God
didn't tell me I should, at least not yet.

So I've really learned to pray much and
listen to the Lord. Above all, I don't want to
hurry my decision making. Two weeks after
Larry died, a friend said, "I'm sure you must be
all rested by now." After two years of caring for
Larry in his illness, in and out of the hospital?
I think not! I need time and space.

God often sends us a friend or two who really understands, empathizes and supports us. It should be the norm for a local church family to stand by with prayer and assistance, but unfortunately that is not always the case. Nor is there a "one size fits all" grieving process. Fran, my childhood friend whose husband died almost a year before mine, wrote of her experience:

> In the early months since Tex died, some of my widowed friends ask me what I *do* to "keep busy." They seem to dash madly about involved in dozens of activities. Well, I see nothing wrong with just sitting still and enjoying a good book or going for a walk with my fat, little dog. I even rediscovered the movies and take in a matinee occasionally. I have coffee with friends, but sometimes I just get lost in my memories. I don't feel guilty about this. I'll know when the right time comes to get busy, and when it does, I will. But until then I will continue to let my heart heal at its own pace.

The goal of the grieving process is to internalize Philippians 3:13, 14 ". . . forgetting what lies behind and reaching forward to what lies ahead, I press on toward the goal for the prize of the upward call of God in Christ Jesus." That gradually works out through:

- ❦ Closing the door *after* resolving any issues from the past.
- ❦ Experiencing healing from negative memories.
- ❦ Opening oneself to relationships which build self-esteem and provide opportunities to help and serve others.

❦ Discovering healthy personhood as a
   single again.
❦ Resuming a meaningful, productive life
   as God directs.

Background props

I tried to understand how my early experiences
with loss could have warped my grief response. Why did
I feel I should helicopter over the grieving process? It may
have been because I lacked role models of good grieving
during my lifetime.

I was only eight when my maternal grandmother
died in midlife. Because I seldom saw her, I did not have
a deep, emotional attachment. We were a loving family,
but I don't recall my mother grieving—not so a child
would notice.

However, I had bonded deeply from babyhood
with my live-in paternal grandmother, Frantiska. She
was my exclusive and beloved caregiver while both my
parents worked. We slept in the same bed since I was an
infant. I was 15 when she died. Given our close bond, I'm
puzzled not to have a single memory about her death and
funeral. Nor do I recall my dad grieving, though he had
been a caring, attentive son. I only remember sitting at
dad's writing desk composing a poem questioning why
life could possibly go on so normally when my beloved
grandmother had just died.

I must have subconsciously missed seeing my
relatives expressing grief. They were serving the traditional after-funeral meal to scores of noisy, laughing
relatives and friends in our dining room.

It seemed to be the practice of our first generation

European immigrant family to go right on with life no matter what calamities took place. Coming from hardy stock, they had seen more than their share of war, separation and tragedies. Immediate adjustment was their way to cope, and the model I saw. The only comment I heard through the years during times of bereavement was speculation about how long someone would take to "get over it."

For some reason, I still feel guilty for not grieving for my dearly loved grandmother who has been in Heaven for more than 55 years.

I vividly recall that a few days after grandmother's death, my parents took me to a furniture store where they let me pick out a new carpet, bedroom suite and desk for grandma's room, which was now to be my own bedroom. I'm sure they stretched themselves financially for that provision.

As an only child, I was especially close to my dad. When he died suddenly in his late fifties, I was already married, living overseas and expecting our second child. Caught up in a busy life of ministry and far away, I don't recall grieving, only experiencing a deep, tender sadness. I lived up to traditional family expectations and went right on with my life. It was two years before I saw mother.

When my mother's father, brother and sister all died suddenly in one year, I saw mother's tears but only at the funerals. Then she bravely went right back to work, adjusting to life alone. Did mother grieve? How? Was she suppressing it? Why? To prove what? To spare whom? I don't know.

I have a flashback to the custom my
parents and extended family carried on.
Every Sunday from spring through fall
they gathered fresh flowers from their
luxuriant gardens and took them to the
Czech cemetery.

From my early childhood, I had to help by discarding old flowers from the previous Sunday, rinsing out the stinky canisters and filling them again with fresh water for new flowers. My parents were careful to equally distribute the bouquets to each grave site of our immediate family members so they would neglect none. They seldom lingered at the cemetery, just quietly attended to the ritual of flowers and went home.

Before winter set in, they cleared each grave of leaves and debris and filled the canisters with artificial flowers, anchoring them with wires to the headstones so they would survive winter's icy blasts and snow.

Memorial Day was always a festive gathering at the cemetery in my Iowa hometown. Relatives met each other at the grave sites, distributed extra lavish bouquets and lingered to chat with one another about family changes during the past year. Memorial Day parades by the veterans of past wars and speeches by city officials were the order of the day.

Perhaps that cemetery ritual was part of their grieving process.

When I traveled to the Czech Republic exploring my ethnic heritage, I was struck with how meticulously they care for grave sites. They plant mini-gardens around the headstones and over the graves, constantly weeding and watering them. I understood how we pass on grief models generationally.

Over the years when my husband's parents and some of his brothers and sisters died, it seemed that Ted never missed a beat. I couldn't tell whether or how he processed his grief because he didn't talk about it. He carried on his ministry as usual.

I was with my mother during her last months of illness in the hospital. After her death, we immediately resumed our busy lives with ministry and our growing family. I loved mother dearly, missed her with a gentle sadness, but I knew nothing about working through any grief. She was buried in Iowa a thousand miles from where we were living and working. I never carried on the flower ritual, though many of my peer cousins still living in my hometown do so.

Therefore, when Ted died, I apparently responded in character based on my past encounters with loss. From the first week after his death, when anyone asked how I was doing, I automatically answered, "Oh, I'm doing fine." I was programmed never to admit I'm not doing O.K. It was my way of holding pain at arm's length, my defense against losing control of my emotions.

After the initial, numbing, shock period following Ted's death, I should normally have begun to work through my grief. I suppressed my emotions, however, convincing myself it was the proper, Christian thing to do. An honest mistake, given my background. I didn't give myself permission to feel pain. I believe it was this concealing of my initial feelings that gave me trouble later.

> I felt that family and friends were looking
> to me to be strong as usual, to put my
> performance where my mouth was regard-
> ing faith in God and personal peace. I
> didn't want to disappoint everyone.

The common hope to quickly "get over it" seems to project a false expectation. I took the "over it" too literally. I bought into the same notion my family had modeled, and my natural, coping temperament kicked in. Now I can understand why I took a helicopter and skimmed over the treetops of the grieving process.

Another reason why I tried to bolt from loss to adjustment and new assignment was because the death of someone close to you makes you keenly aware of your own mortality. I was gripped with the thought that my own "finish line" might also be near. How could I afford (I thought) to spend time in any phantom grieving process which would take time to work through? I felt an urgency to live and work even faster than I had been.

I know that I can lose myself in my work. It seems to give my life meaning. I needed to prove that I was still alive, alert, capable and useful. I subconsciously, and wrongly, linked my productivity to my self-worth.

Reentering the grieving process

My well-meaning Christian comforters may have contributed to pushing me to premature adjustment. I am concerned that we Christians are sometimes not realistic about death, glossing over the pain of it, pretending it won't happen to us. Therefore, "getting over it" quickly is a false idea we fall into. What I really needed was simply *permission to grieve,* to freely express my emotions in that initial period.

Some people will try to spare you from grieving. They will not intend to do so, nor even realize they are doing so. You may not realize this is being done to you, but the effort will be there—subtle but very effective. It is sometimes done by too many words.

It is as though people think they have to defend God in grief. As soon as tragedy comes, people tend to crank up an inexhaustible supply of philosophical statements trying to explain it all. I guess they feel if they can explain it, the grief will go away. . . . But there are no philosophical answers to explain the tragedies of life. No one can understand why these are there, much less explain them. Trying to do so neither explains nor comforts.[3]

The tendency for people to talk too much when trying to comfort a friend is sensitively described in a poem by Ruth Bell Graham in *The Christian Writer* magazine:

> Don't talk to me yet;
> The wound is fresh,
> the nauseous pain
> I can't forget
> fades into numbness
> like a wave,
> then comes again.

Your tears I understand,
but grief is deaf;
it cannot hear the words
you gently planned
and tried to say.
But . . .
pray.

Comforters don't say so, but they often leave the impression that if your grief lingers, your faith is weak. You feel under pressure to recover quickly to prove your faith. You redouble your efforts to hide what you feel, not admit it. Loss of a loved one is a major wound that doesn't heal overnight. You need time and support until you heal.

I hear accounts of folks giving testimonies in church about how they have won the victory over grief only weeks after a tragedy. I feel sad. In almost every case the person has not felt free to grieve. To not feel free means there must be a denial of grief. To deny means it must be swallowed. To swallow grief means you are going to be sick. Swallowed feelings do not go away. They surface as illness, nervousness, tension, and depression.

To get over grief in a hurry does not mean you are superior. To take a long time does not mean you are weak. Quick recovery does not mean you did not love. Long recovery does not mean you did love.[4]

When I finally took the backward dive to become a *grief processor* two years into my widowhood, I began to feel as if I had been put into a *food processor*. When I finally expressed my emotions, in private, they were all chopped up, ground and pulverized. The emotions I expressed were ones I had become accustomed to controlling.

Whatever it would take, I was finally gently and properly advised, I should free my emotions. However deep I would have to dig, I should exhume my normal, legitimate feelings. It didn't matter how long ago I buried them. I should find them. It would be all right if some of them ran away and didn't come back. If some kept returning, I should welcome them back *for a while* until I had dealt with them.

I could hardly believe the extent to which I became immobilized when I first reentered the grieving process! I was in unfamiliar territory. I found myself slipping into the "Slough of Despond," getting sucked under. My feelings of isolation and loneliness became intense. I felt I was losing ground rather than progressing. I suddenly lost confidence in myself. My depression threw me into a totally unproductive, lethargic state. Day after day I felt useless. Time passed and I couldn't seem to catch it as it went by. Things I had enthusiastically pursued left me flat.

Because I had falsely tied my self-worth to producing, when I couldn't even continue writing, I struggled for my identity.

Then, at the opposite extreme of the emotional spectrum, I began *feeling,* at last, giving myself permission to hurt. The pain was fresh because I had not fully expressed it before. Who would want to deliberately step back into that kind of trauma? Granted, it is easier to keep suppressing painful feelings than to make your way through them. It would have been easier on me, certainly preferable, to accept and embrace my emotions *initially* and keep moving on normally, gradually through the process toward adjustment. However, if I did skip the process the first time, going back and through it was better. Otherwise I would continually keep bumping over potholes and never reach the smoother freeway of adjustment.

I knew that God didn't intend for me to stay in that introspective mode. It was an indispensable journey, but a temporary one. I knew God was working on me, purging me from the pride of thinking I didn't need to experience normal grief. I had not realized that I was not pleasing Him by trying to skip a grieving process that He had provided for my welfare.

Jesus was called "a man of sorrows, acquainted with grief" (Isaiah 53:3). Grief and sorrow were not His predominant nature, but they had a vital part in His experience. He was "acquainted" with grief, fully tasting it as part of the human condition so He could sustain and comfort us in our human grief.

Why did Jesus weep at the death of His friend Lazarus? We can only speculate. More than anyone, Jesus knew what lay beyond death for one who entered the presence of His Father. In His humanity, Jesus may have given expression to the grief of earthly separation, to see the effects of man's fallen nature. Illness and deterioration are negative parts of human experience no one can escape. Perhaps He wept to realize that if He raised His friend, Lazarus would have to go through the dying process twice. Whatever the reasons, if Jesus wept, He grants me permission to grieve.

God was showing me that He provides the human emotion of grief to help my healing and recovery, that I would come out on the other side a complete, whole person. My grief time was only a necessary season. I needed to fully experience this stage both for my future well-being and to empathize compassionately with my singled out friends who suffer similar losses. I needed to learn how to "weep with those who weep" and experience how blessed it really is to mourn and to be called the children of God. (Matthew 5:4)

Only as I wrestle with real feelings of grief do I come forth with stronger faith muscles. Then it will have been *creative grief.* David wrote in Psalm 23, "Yea, though I walk through the valley of the shadow of death . . . ." *"Walk through"* is a key phrase. Walking through the grieving process is what healthy, good grief is all about.

My valley of grieving then becomes a Valley of Learning.

Valley of Learning
(A Paraphrase of Psalm 23)

Lord, You are my guide and teacher;
I will not be afraid.
I walk a fearful tightrope no longer.
You fill my world with meaning:

The clouds and sunlight make trees
speak truth.
You put me with people who open their
arms to me,
who open their minds and hearts.
We talk back and forth.
Even though I pass through terrible times,
I am not afraid,
because Your presence, Lord, is with me.
I feel it sometimes like an arm
across my shoulders.
You prepare for me the food I need;
Your hands heal my wounds
and I am filled with gratitude.
Surely this world is the home of the Lord,
And I delight to discover You in it;
and I will hope to learn more of You
whatever may come to me hereafter.[5]

Oh, how much one can learn in that valley! My friend, Sandra, recalled her experience as she looked back on her first year without her husband.

I'm not the same person I was a year ago. Life will never be the same. I hope I'm kinder and more understanding, with more compassion and sympathy for others. One of the first things I learned was not to sweat the small stuff. I can't believe how much time I used to waste fretting over trivial things. But no more.

Watching a beautiful sunset is so much more important than the urgency of doing the dinner dishes. There's no one else around to see whether they are done "on time" or not.

I attended many meetings for survivors sponsored by Hospice. I don't know what I would have done without Hospice helpers during Jack's last months. I found it a real help to meet with others who were going through the same thing.

When I was with them I didn't feel the need to be strong and keep a stiff upper lip. They encouraged me to take my time to go through the grieving process. We were all in the same boat—we could laugh together, cry together and be perfectly honest about our feelings. I don't attend as many meetings anymore. I feel I've moved on to a different stage.

*O*ur hearts break and our lives heal in distinctive ways that mark each of us as unique. Yet, through sighs and tears, we speak a universal language that marks all of us as human.

Grief Sounds [1]

Don't Push Me Through the "Stage" Door!

 **3**

early every book I read about the loss of a loved one invariably sent me, along with every other widow, through the so-called "grief stages." I was told:

- There is nothing neat and orderly about stages of grief.
- You don't graduate from one stage to the next.
- You're not promoted at the end because there really isn't an end.
- There are no doors to enter or leave a stage.
- Feelings experienced in any stage may mingle with the feelings of another stage.
- You may leapfrog over one stage, then have to return to it.
- You don't experience the stages in sequence.
- The duration of each may vary.
- You may feel as if you are in a maze, often facing blank walls.
- You may doubt you'll ever find your way out— but you will.

I find "stages" a misleading word. To call them phases or steps isn't quite accurate either. All such terms imply defined periods. It may be a matter of semantics, but I prefer to call them *universal grief feelings.* You may experience them all at once. Sometimes you can't distinguish one feeling from another. I use the term *grief feelings* for what most books call "stages," but where the word is used in quoted material, I let it stand.

They suggest different lists of grief feelings. The following is one list: Numbness, Shock, Denial, Anger, Disorientation (the crazies), Depression, Guilt, Panic, Acceptance and Renewal. Such feelings are thought to be common to nearly all grievers. While considering them, we must make room for individual temperaments and specific situations.

> Our hearts break and our lives heal in distinctive ways that mark each of us as unique. Yet, through sighs and tears, we speak a universal language that marks all of us as human. . . . The grieving process includes some predictable feelings and behavior. Grieving is painful. Successful recovery from grief requires more than time, but it does take time. Rushing does not complete the process any sooner. Nor does suppression of grief. To ignore grief or to postpone dealing with it intensifies the pain and hinders a person's ability to live fully.[1]

Elisabeth Elliot stated that she didn't even hear about "grief work" and the so-called stages of grief until years after her first bereavement. She wasn't sure whether going through the stages was necessary for all, but that if she had heard of them at the time, she might have felt obliged to move consciously through them. She wrote:

> Perhaps my memory of the early months of my widowhood is selective, but I am sure that in spite of very real grief God met me in ways psychology knows nothing about. He gave me peace which was quite beyond explanation, and at time an exuberance of joy that was, as Scripture confirms, "unspeakable." Thomas á Kempis knew the simpler way, "a pure and whole forsaking of ourselves and of our own will, that we might get freedom of spirit."
>
> The stages of grief work may be unavoidable if we feel ourselves adrift in a universe without meaning, but may there not be some shortcuts to peace for those who truly believe in the Shepherd, and go gently with Him through the Valley of the Shadow?[2]

The value of considering common grief feelings is that it helps you understand that they are normal and reassures you that you will recover, heal and become a whole person again.

Let's understand that so-called grief stages may be reflections of culture and society, even ethnic in expression. In other than Western societies, the stages, as such, may be unknown. They expect an entirely different response from a widow. She may have little choice on how to handle the death of her husband. We may be shocked to think about it, but in certain cultures even today they bury a widow alive with her dead husband! Without a husband, society regards her as obsolete, a nonperson.

Our Western society seems to expect the stages of grieving, perhaps because death is usually not dealt with openly. We tend to live our lives as though they are not terminal. When death comes, it takes us by surprise. We don't prepare for the inevitable.

Stages of grieving? I don't think my mother, as part of her generation, knew about such stages when my dad died. My grandmother in Europe didn't know about stages she should go through after grandfather died before he was 40 and left her with six young children to raise. After the simple burial, she went right back to the potato fields.

Let's not look at culture, society or customs in the East or West. Let's look at Scripture. Are the stages of grief valid for the Christian? I resisted the need for them in the early months of my loss because I viewed them as defined periods I would have to go through, and some of them seemed unchristian to me.

Some friends advised, "Everyone must go through those stages." They offered sympathy for all the struggles I'd have to go through before I "came out of it." Others predicted I would pick myself right up as if my world had not turned upside down. I favored the latter scenario because going through all those stages scared me.

Neither scenario turned out to fit me. Ultimately I had to find my own way through the unfamiliar maze of my loss—and so do you. Each of us responds and adjusts differently, but perhaps you might benefit from my misunderstanding and mistakes.

Because I thought of the grieving process in stages, I defined them too narrowly, and proudly thought I had more answers than I really did. I found out I was not "superlady" after all. Now I have traded compassion for knowing all the answers. To help others, I must assume the attitude, "Don't walk behind me—I may not lead you aright. Walk beside me, and let us learn together."

Foggy twilight

How merciful the Lord is to us singled out women to provide a vague, gentle fog to surround us immediately after our husband's death, keeping the activity and noise level at arm's length! In the first week, I felt like a robot going through the motions without emotions. God granted that blessed buffer so I could make it through all the responsibilities and decisions suddenly forced upon me. Some of my singled out friends describe this as being on automatic pilot, and most of them have experienced it.

This gentle shock absorber was like the Lord's comforting arms around me. It was a natural shutdown of what could have been panic—God's "comfort zone" was presided over by the Comforter, the Holy Spirit. A storm was truly raging around me, but I didn't feel the full force of the turbulence.

It was as if I were in the eye of the storm, feeling deep peace. Lifted above into the heavenlies, it seemed as if my feet barely skimmed the ground. I was resting in the Lord's control and somehow anesthetized from the immediate pain. It felt as though I were in a protective bubble, insulated from the real world around me.

Some measure of that initial cushion period is experienced even by widowed friends who are part of "those who have no hope" in Christ. *Nevertheless, I want to give the glory to the Lord* who dispenses that heavenly tranquilizer by His Holy Spirit, don't you?

In that tender fog I was able to make all the funeral arrangements, write a tribute to my husband and prepare his life story in print for two memorial services that first week. I even shopped for some personal clothing, went to the supermarket for provisions as usual, arranged for out-of-town guests and phoned relatives and friends at a distance. Of course I leaned on the generous and willing help of my precious family and friends. The Lord provided them as helpers in His comfort zone.

However, I don't remember much about that first week or so. Did I do it in a dream?

I had a vague feeling that reality and pain would eventually catch up with me, but for that initial period I reveled in what the Bible calls the "peace that passes understanding" supplied by my caring Lord. I had similar sweet times wrapped in God's gentle fog in the months afterward when things got hectic, and I needed shelter. Thank God for His protecting shield!

The time eventually comes when we must emerge from that refuge and squarely face our emotions. The Comforter doesn't abandon us at that point but stays with us as we deal with the past and encounter what's ahead.

Denying denial

I was positive *I* wouldn't go through a *denial* stage. My childhood friend, Fran, wrote about spending so much time searching for Leo. "I would drive by our favorite restaurant and look for his pickup in the parking lot. And past the barber shop or the hardware store. It just seemed as if he had to be somewhere, even though I knew he was gone."

In the early days after his death, denying that one's spouse has really died may be a survival mechanism, an attempt to ease the emotional blow from the end of a close relationship. After the first shock of Ted's sudden death, I was keenly aware of his absence. I'm a realist—I never denied that my loss took place. I assumed that was all that people meant by "the denial stage."

Denial, however, is not simply refusing to believe that death has taken place. Eventually I realized that denial also means refusing to acknowledge my own emotions or expressing them. Thinking that I didn't need to go through the grieving process was a serious form of denial. I expressed that by repeating, "I'm O.K. My husband is celebrating in Heaven."

Denial is sometimes closely bound to guilt, often hard to distinguish. One aspect is to put a halo on our spouse, crown him with sainthood and bury my memories of his shortcomings. More rarely for Christians, some attribute to him nothing but faults and inadequacies, and deny our own imperfections in marriage.

Some use a benign amnesia which enables them to canonize the person. However, a halo over a dead family member could cast shadows of unmerited guilt on survivors who didn't measure up as the spouse, sibling, parent or offspring of a saint. Most of us, however, can identify ourselves as members of a family that needed many apologies and frequent forgiveness, but which, overall, had much cause for grateful love. The same kind of realism will equip us to face frankly what still calls for repentance and reconciliation among us.[3]

Books on grief point out that women tend to attach those halos in the presence of others and in their own minds for various reasons. Sometimes, they tell us, we try to cover up poor relationships or failings in our marriages. We feel we must shore up our husband's virtues. We create myths about our husbands which those who knew them well might find unrealistic.

One author suggested we should privately list all the *good* points we can recall about our husbands. When we have exhausted the good points, we should list his *less than perfect* characteristics, habits and traits, even character flaws and failings. No one will see that list.

I tried it. The first list was easy. I made a long list of all the admirable, commendable, praiseworthy qualities "Saint Ted" possessed. Sweet, positive memories were easier to handle emotionally, though they evoked tears of missing him. I felt warm inside remembering what I appreciated in him, even eulogizing him.

I dragged my feet about the second list. Somehow it seemed sacrilegious to criticize the departed. I wrestled with denial again, but understood that this wasn't criticizing. Reluctantly I continued. Some things I put down I would never have told him face to face, and would not admit to others. More likely, I would have covered up for him. Suddenly, there it was—all hanging out, down in black and white in my own handwriting. Both lists were longer than I thought possible. I went repeatedly over my two lists.

I began to feel a freedom to accept my husband as the fully human, truly lovable man he was. In some sense, I was demythologizing him. He was a fine man, but he wasn't perfect.

I married a sinner who was saved by God's grace, and he married a sinful wife saved by grace. Both of us had our faults and failings. I don't need to hold an imaginary halo over my husband's head. *Now he is perfect, in the perfection of Christ, in the presence of Christ.* While on earth, even as a Christian, he was simply human. So am I. I don't need to be reminded of that.

Because of this exercise, I realized I had not yet processed forgiveness of the less-than-perfect Ted, nor had I forgiven myself for shortcomings and sins during our marriage. Therefore, I made a determined though painful effort to make still another list.

Specifically, I put down things Ted did, perhaps unintentionally, that hurt me, and the things that, in my eyes, he failed to do during our long marriage. I faced the things he did that I felt were wrong, inadvisable, irritating—things which frustrated me. (A marriage of 45 years can accumulate quite a list!)

After serious self-examination, I made another list of what could have been, in *his* eyes, *my* shortcomings and failings, things that probably vexed and disappointed him about me. I was painfully honest and precise in spelling these out. My list turned out to be twice as long as the one with his "transgressions!" As the scroll of more than four decades of our life together unrolled, my need for *receiving* forgiveness for multitudes of weighty commissions and omissions became staggering, almost oppressive.

Why in the world should I dredge up all that? My husband was dead. Surely, considering the perfection and glories of Life on the Other Side, such things wouldn't bother him now!

Still, I realized that some of them still bothered *me* because I live with their consequences. I had to admit to some roots of bitterness in my memory garden. They were *my* excess baggage, weights still besetting me. They translated into unresolved guilt and anger—at myself, most of all, only residually at Ted. They were not things I should keep dwelling on for the rest of my life, interfering with my peace of mind and holding me back from my new assignment from the Lord. They would remain to fester and poison me *if I didn't deal with them once for all.*

What can I do about them now? I can no longer confess my shortcomings face to face to my husband. I can't communicate with the dead. Ted's death marked the end of all my chances to change my ways, to make up for my sins of omission and commission, my neglects and regrets. How can I receive my husband's forgiveness? How can he express to me his need to be forgiven?

I went directly to the Lord with all those needs. I confessed them as honestly and completely as I knew how. I asked the Lord to forgive me for my list and any additions He knows about. Then I affirmed my whole-hearted forgiveness of my husband for the things I thought he would ask forgiveness.

Finally, I laid all the lists before the Lord. I literally lit a match to them and claimed God's promise that *once for all, both of us have forgiven each other, and God has forgiven us.* "If we confess our sins, He is faithful and righteous to forgive us our sins and to cleanse us from all unrighteousness" (1 John 1:9). Our status is now pristine, as if we had never transgressed or hurt each other. Guilt is wiped away. I don't need to carry such excess baggage any longer. Jesus said, "My yoke is easy, my burden is light." I have laid aside the weight of unresolved guilt.

Finally it was time to bury both "Saint Ted" and "Less-than-perfect-Ted." It was time to forgive him and accept forgiveness for myself for being less than perfect. It was time to receive God's forgiveness *for all things in the past.*

A guilt stage?

I thought I was finished with guilt. I started by declaring *Not guilty!* Surely I wouldn't need to linger in any guilt stage. Moreover, I was sure I could skip the stage of anger. Again, I defined both guilt and anger too narrowly. The *New World Dictionary* defines guilt as "a painful feeling of self-reproach resulting from a belief that one has done something wrong or immoral."

> [Guilt is] . . . the yukkiest, thickest, most pervasive, saddest feeling in the world . . . . The black, sinuous substance of guilt sneaks up on us with animal cunning. It settles its pulsing flesh upon us and hisses and spits and tears.[4]

Nevertheless, countless "if onlys" were still lingering around bothering me until I felt I was knee-deep in that mucky guilt. Yes, I had dealt with major giving and receiving of forgiveness. There were still residual aspects of guilt I needed to face and then deal with before I could move on to full healing. One author described it:

> Guilt is a natural response to death's wound. All of us hurt the person we love, one way or another: we say sharp words, are inconsiderate and impatient, act selfishly. In life we have a chance to straighten things out with, "I'm sorry, please forgive me," with gifts and surprises and special acts of love. Death closes the door on making amends, opens the door to a flood of "If only. . . " thoughts.
> Many people who feel most guilty have been almost completely loving toward the person who died, and have no reason for guilt. The person who does not experience forgiveness, who continues, after months of acute grief, to be filled with "Why didn't I?" thoughts, is in a potentially dangerous situation and should talk with a pastor or religious advisor.[5]

I had a flashback of guilt because I didn't get up and check on Ted when I thought I heard two voices murmuring low in conversation in his room around three a.m. at what may have been his time of death. (Was it his guardian angel sent to let him know his course on earth was finished, and that he would accompany him on his incredibly exciting trip Home into the presence of Jesus?) Still half asleep, I planned to tease Ted in the morning about talking in his sleep, as he was in the habit of doing. The murmur of voices was not like an argument or crying out for help—more like the sharing of a happy secret.

Still, why didn't I check on him? My fuzzy reasoning at the time was that he wouldn't have wanted me to wake him if he were talking in his sleep. *What if I had done so?*

Guilt? I didn't cause my husband's death, nor could I have done anything to prevent it. "Our times are in His [God's] hands," not in ours. I don't have the keys of life and death. My husband died according to God's time. I don't understand it but even our "accidents" are in the providential plan of God. I knew I shouldn't slip into the mire of personal false guilt feelings. Christ paid the penalty to forgive all my guilt including any vestiges of *real or imagined* guilt.

Sincere regrets? Of course. Regret is normal hindsight. It is different from guilt which is remorse over behavior or neglect for which we *can* personally blame ourselves—a deliberate act. Ted and I pledged our lives to each other "for better or worse." Many things could have been worse. Many things could have been better—both on my part and his. I don't think God wants us to slosh around in the guilt of self-reproach.

Later, other guilt inciters flashed through my mind. Why didn't I set aside my writing more often to make time for us to go swimming in the indoor pool at the recreation center? Ted seemed to be in good health when he died, but perhaps he would have been in even better physical condition if I had not been so busy, and we had gone swimming more often. Being somewhat older, he had already retired but I had not.

While wading around in my guilt, I took a memory trip back many years. I discovered old guilt feelings that were still simmering on some back burners of my mind and emotions. How about my transgressions, neglects, omissions, unintentional though they were, *against other loved ones in the past?* And their offenses against me— imagined or real?

Can I possibly resolve the still-lurking
guilt I've now unearthed from long ago?
Does it matter if the people are no longer
living? What can I do about it now?

After many weeks at my mother's bedside in the hospital, I wasn't present when she died. I still feel guilty about that. Mother was paralyzed from strokes and couldn't speak. She seemed to be trying desperately to say something, but no matter what I mentioned, asking whether that was what she wanted to say, her eyes filled with tears, and she would shake her head no. I've been carrying guilt all these years for not pressing the matter further, for not trying even harder to understand her. I still carry the guilt of not being sensitive to my mother's emotions and needs after the death of my dad. Why didn't I sit and talk with mother about her loneliness and distress and comfort her?

I feel guilty because I wasn't there emotionally for my beloved grandma when her daughter, my aunt, died of a sudden rare illness. Looking back, I imagine how I must have ignored and disappointed her during her time of sorrow. After bonding so closely with her during my early childhood, where was I when she needed me?

During grandma's prolonged illness I recall that I was a preoccupied young teen absorbed in exciting school activities, spending all my time with friends—doubtless quite a normal teen. Grandma died within a year after her daughter's death. The only entry in my daily dairy for her entire last year was that I saw grandma crying and saying she felt that she was just a burden, that nobody needed or wanted her anymore. Why does that memory still bring tears to my eyes after nearly 60 years?

Can I receive forgiveness for those things *even now, so late?* For other unresolved baggage from the past which keeps going round and round my memory carousel like unclaimed airline baggage?

Based on God's faithfulness, His promises have no expiration date. They carry an eternal guarantee. So I dealt with the guilt of long ago events in the same way as I belatedly dealt with the excess baggage of guilt from my marriage. I took them one by one to the foot of the Cross, received God's forgiveness, and left them there.

Guilt of other kinds

Some of my other singled out friends had different circumstances in their marriages and wrestle with their own special brand of guilt.

Monica felt guilty because she felt free from the bondage of a husband who, although a professing Christian, had physically abused her all their married life. She felt guilty because she didn't feel "the usual kind of grief" at the passing of "a beloved companion."

Sandra felt guilty because her feelings are more like relief from more than 20 years of looking after a physically and mentally deteriorating husband suffering from a progressively debilitating disease. Her own health suffered while she sacrificially provided that care. She put her life totally on hold. Her guilt was compounded because she had flashbacks about some times of impatience with his weakness and helpless condition.

Margo felt secretly happy when her husband died because she is now legitimately out of a miserable marriage she entered on a rebound from another relationship. She admits privately that she was running from the Lord when she made that decision. To her credit, she stuck with him, but felt guilty about her decades of cover-up, and now about her pretense of grief when she doesn't feel any for the death of a man she never loved.

Belle, a missionary wife who lost her husband in a plane crash when they were both in their mid-forties with six children to raise, slipped into nearly a year of deep depression and could hardly function. In the years following, she felt guilty for not having been the victorious role model she thought people expected of her to be. She had been angry with God because she felt He deserted her. She wouldn't even pray, and decided to leave Christian work. God was compassionate and loving to her, patient, ever-present with her, and eventually her depression lifted. She went on to faithfully raise her children and continued in Christian ministry. Nevertheless, Belle continued to feel guilty about that early dark period.

Cathy felt guilty because she couldn't grieve. For 30 years she lived with a secret alcoholic who mistreated their children and carried on one affair after another, blatantly ignoring Cathy's feelings and flaunting his extramarital relationships. She put up with years of his addiction to pornography, while he hypocritically held the position of deacon in their church to enhance his professional career.

Wanda felt guilty for praying for her husband's death after he was fatally injured in an auto accident. He lay in a coma, sustained by life support. When he died from his injuries within a few weeks of the accident, Wanda felt guilty because she thought she "pulled a spiritual plug" by praying for his death and his relief from suffering.

Nedra, whose young missionary husband suffered a sudden heart attack and died, carried guilt for years because she argued with her husband over some trivial matter the night before he died. Although he had a congenital heart condition that would have led to his early death anyway, she believed she contributed to his stress and somehow caused his death.

Guilt feelings can be as diverse as the kinds of marriages. True guilt and imagined or false guilt are often hard to distinguish. Most of us feel some of each kind. Some things we have knowingly done or failed to do, and other things we could really not have done anything about. God's grace is sufficient for both kinds of guilt. One author wrote:

So many people struggle with guilt in their lives. When victorious Christians exclaim, "God has completely removed all my guilt!"

hosts of other struggling Christians quietly respond, "Yeah, easy for you to say. You don't know how guilty I am!" *But you don't know how forgiven you are!* Do you struggle with guilt for past sins? God's mercy will help you eradicate that guilt from your life and move ahead to becoming the person God wants you to be.[6]

Bubbling cauldron of anger

My friend, Barbara, wrote me about her anger at losing her husband.

I was *so* angry at Ron for going away and leaving me here alone! And mad at my poor, feeble 89 year old neighbor for still being alive when my big, strong, handsome Ron is gone. And yes, mad at God for letting this terrible lung cancer happen to us. Mad at Ron because he wouldn't stop smoking even though he knew it was ruining his health.

Well, *I* didn't expect to go through an anger stage. I'm not angry by nature. Again I defined the feeling too narrowly. I assumed anger at one's spouse for dying was the main issue. How could I be angry with Ted? He didn't want to die yet. He had many plans for our future together. He didn't choose to leave me alone.

I just couldn't be angry at God. I've always believed that whatever He allows is for good. Nevertheless, I didn't realize what a bubbling cauldron of unresolved anger I concealed toward medical personnel. Anger is seldom logical—it aims at any target available. With a magnifying glass I went over and over the circumstances surrounding Ted's death. I was angry at his doctor for promising to come to the hospital and determine cause of death and then never showing up. Our sons were equally angry. We were angry because the doctor didn't phone or make any effort to talk with any of us about my husband's death. I wanted some assurance that he had done all he could for my husband's health. The doctor simply didn't communicate with me. Nor did he give me any advice or medical help when I was experiencing anxiety and physical symptoms during that time.

I was angry at the hospital where Ted was taken after his death because they didn't get in touch with me about my wishes, not even asking whether I wanted an autopsy. I was angry at the mortuary for making major errors in the newspaper notice after they took down all the accurate information, angry at the church where we had been worshiping for not being there for me.

I felt hurt and angry that it took six weeks after my husband's death (hopefully not typical of the experience of other widows) for the minister to visit me. His "stopping by" eventually, he explained, was because he was on his way to an appointment nearby. "I know we'll see you in church when you're finally ready," were his parting words. Little comfort!

I was angry at certain people, supposedly good friends, whom I had repeatedly helped in *their* time of need, who totally seemed to ignore my loss.

I was angry at Ted's lack of forethought by neglecting to make advance arrangements in case of death.

I repressed all that anger (denial, again) because anger "wasn't Christian." Nevertheless, anger will find a way out, whether or not we acknowledge it. Some feel their anger is justified when directed at the illness, accident or circumstances leading to death. That's understandably a human response.

The Christian husband of one of my friends was struck and killed by a fast-moving truck on the highway as he stopped to help a stranded motorist. We can't pretend to understand why God should have allowed that to happen. Nevertheless, we should steadfastly trust God and believe that He only allows what is for our ultimate good and His glory. As our Creator, He gave us the capacity for anger. God may not be as concerned with the *fact* of our anger, as He is with what we *do* about it.

In the same way as I dealt with my baggage of guilt related to my husband, I had to deal with my feelings of anger toward those whom I felt had let me down or offended me in the days and weeks after Ted's death. I told the Lord aloud that I was forgiving them, mentioning them by name. Then I deliberately recalled the positives, the good, comforting, supportive and loving things so many people had done at that time. I was finally able to thank God for everything.

After that I felt purged, cleansed, free of pretense or hypocrisy. The past was past with its regrets and could-have-done-betters. As an imperfect child of God, I should press on to try pleasing the Lord for the rest of my life. Imperfect, but forgiven.

Unfortunately, I went through that major
part of the grieving process later than I
should have—two years later—but better
late than never.

It was not necessary or healthy for me to keep walking back through that process again. Having resolved my feelings, I finally closed the door. God invited me to walk with Him through new doors and into His plans for my future.

The depression pit

Surely not a temptation *for me.* Depression *really* didn't seem compatible with the Christian way, therefore I planned to skip it. As an outgoing, sociable, usually "up" person, I wouldn't even be tempted to isolate myself. To my dismay, I went through such dark seasons of depression that none of my family or friends would have believed. I hid my low feelings behind a coping facade because "it was the right thing to do." For a considerable time I did have to force myself to be with people, preferring to stay home alone.

Depression is more than just a blue mood, more than sadness. It often begins with uneasiness, restlessness, then lethargy. It is more like a fog drifting over and gradually clouding the atmosphere of our lives. It distorts our vision. If allowed to continue, illness may result. Insomnia, dizziness and headaches, even a heaviness in the chest can develop—real or imagined. Low self-esteem often accompanies it. Some women lose total interest in life, and some even have a death wish. A thorough medical check up is the place to start if any such symptoms persist. It is important not to hide during periods of depression, but be with people, especially friends, at least part of the time.

Some depression is without cause, some arises from good reasons. We who are widows do have a reason—we have suffered a major life loss. Because our resistance is down, we are more susceptible to illness. But we can work through our vulnerability with the Lord's help. I realized that I should not blame myself for my weakness. I should cut myself some slack, not try to be so "together."

Studies have shown that even weather contributes to depression. I found that dull, gray days spread a pall over my spirit. I feel the effect of S.A.D. (Seasonal Affective Disorder) on my spirits each year. The anniversary of Ted's death coincides with the onset of winter. Gloomy skies and the humdrum of winter begin to settle in. The chill November wind blows leaves from trees. Shorter days and the lack of sunshine are linked to altered brain chemistry and depression, they tell us. People tend to have low energy and are less productive. Researchers tell us that some are so seasonally depressed they can hardly function, lacking power to concentrate. Even routine decisions and common tasks consume an unusual amount of energy.

I recognized that my depression was in part because I began to live alone for the first time in my life. Yes, I did want solitude, but I got too lonely. I wanted to be with people, yet I couldn't wait to get home. I was ashamed to admit, "I don't want to live alone. I really *don't* like it." I masked my true feelings because I didn't want it to look like I did not accept the circumstances God was giving me. I tried to convince myself, and insisted especially to my family, that I was eager and happy to start living alone, that I looked forward to open-ended time for writing and following my own schedule.

Who was I kidding? To leap from a lifetime of living with other people to a life of "solitary confinement" was traumatic. I'm an outgoing, relational person. I grew up in a close-knit family. When I graduated from high school I moved into a college dorm, then into marriage after graduation, followed by more than two decades of raising a houseful of four, noisy boys. After that, more years in the empty nest but with the companionship of my husband.

I rationalized my desire to live alone now, albeit in idyllic circumstances for my writing career. I attempted to do it without a transition period and without taking time to work through the grieving process.

When we travel through the darkness of depression, let's understand that it is preparing us for a better future, and that in time the clouds will lift. The sun will shine again, and roses will bloom in season. The perspective of one author helped me to cope:

> [Depression] will change you in a way that you cannot understand. You will survive despite your weakness. How you spend your time while sailing the blackness doesn't really matter. What matters is that you keep sailing, and that you never deny your pain.
>
> Face it as best you can. You can accept your pain or you can curse it, but never deny it. Your honesty is the invisible star that will lead you into the dawn. So be good to yourself. And simply wait. Every midnight has its morning. Yours, too, will come. [7]

No panic buttons for me!

A panic stage? Finally I could skip that stage! After all, the Lord promised to take care of me. Being alone couldn't be that bad. After the initial trauma of

Ted's death, I fully expected to keep the lid on my emotions and experience God's perfect peace.

It wasn't to be. Physical and emotional anxiety/panic attacks over which I had no control stalked me intermittently even beyond the first year. Struggling to learn to live alone took its toll and contributed to my apprehension and tension. When in a panic mode, I wanted to withdraw and avoid people.

Some call this period "the crazies" and find themselves thinking and doing irrational things. They seriously begin to wonder whether they are going off the deep end. They think perhaps they are cracking up or falling apart. It frightens them. This is another feeling that most of us experience to a greater or lesser degree. Unfortunately, some women going through this irrational period make decisions they later regret. Some uproot their families and move too soon, others make bad financial decisions, still others jump into shaky relationships, on impulse marry again, or are victims of exploiters.

This phase, too, will pass. We will make it.
Someone suggested we keep affirming: *I
am normal* although my life seems to be
in turmoil right now. My feelings are
jumbled, my future is uncertain, but *I am
normal.* God and I can work this out. I
can survive!

F. Scott Fitzgerald expressed it dramatically: "In a real dark night of the soul, it is always three o'clock in the morning." Most of us find nighttime to be the most difficult. All emotions are exaggerated—but dawn will come. "My soul waiteth for the Lord more than they that watch for the morning" (Psalm 130:6).

Morning

Dawn at last . . .
fragrant as Honeysuckle
welcomed with relief
approaching silently
on the coattails
of my nervous night
when I lay
gripped by panic
rigid with fright
confronting personal ghosts
wrestling with memories
heart pounding thunderous tattoos
eyes darting in the darkness
searching for a pinpoint of light.
Dawn at last!
a fresh page and virgin day.
God saw me through! [8]

A friend who knew the pain and disorientation of panic feelings suggested that when we are depressed or panic grips us, we should be extra kind to ourselves. We should not set an unrealistically high standard for ourselves, but just be satisfied to muddle through. Not everyone can be organized and sensible when they are in pain or groping through the darkness. Muddling through is as good a strategy as any, if it works for you.

Acceptance is not a stage

In my first draft of this book, I thought everything was simpler than it turned out to be. I proposed that if Christians who have suffered the loss of a loved one would *begin* with acceptance rather than expect acceptance to be the *final* stage, as many grief counselors suggest, the grieving process might not even be necessary.

I was only partly right. Acceptance from the beginning is best, but it isn't the end. It doesn't cancel the need for the grieving process. We should cultivate the attitude of "Yes, Lord" acceptance and thanks for whatever God brings or allows in our lives. That confidence stems from our assurance that God has our best interests at heart. Putting it into practice, when I first realize that my spouse died, I should affirm my trust in God's goodness and plan. However, it will still take time for my emotions to catch up with what my faith has affirmed, to trickle my trust into my emotions. But I will be on the right track.

Many singled out women, however, arrive at acceptance later. My friend Joyce shared her experience with me:

I am in my second year of widowhood. With trembling steps I think I'm entering the stage of acceptance and healing now. I have many setbacks, but I can now smile through my tears, and memories are starting to bring comfort instead of pain. Lonely for Bud? Oh yes. Missing him? Always. But instead of demanding to know why this happened, I am finally beginning to say, "Thank you, God, for all those years we *did* have." I can never lose those joys.

It has taken me this whole long, bitter, painful year to get to this point.

Death's sting is real, although it is no longer lethal. That sting is what makes my grief real. Part of the acceptance is to embrace the pain and go through the grieving experience. As I give myself permission to feel, I maintain my touch with reality. I don't feign bravado. My courage grows with my ascent out of and through my pain. Slowly but surely I recognize I'm moving toward adjustment.

To accept my lot as appointed by God is to perceive it as good, *acceptable* and perfect (Romans 8:28,29) and part of God's process to conform me to the image of Jesus. Acceptance is like an engine drawing me along the track toward God's goal for me. Not accepting my feelings of grief and pain is like shunting myself off on a side track. I'm stalled from moving on through grief at a normal pace.

Thank you, Lord, for doing all things well. Even this. You are good. Your timing, Your ways are beyond my understanding. Nevertheless, I choose to accept what has happened as Your perfect plan for Ted and for me. I choose to praise You for it. I choose not to resist or rebel against Your ways.

Now I look to You to give me abundant grace and strength for my personal pain. Give me wisdom and direction so I can adjust to my new life. I trust You for courage. I anticipate Your new assignment.

Open hands should characterize the soul's attitude toward God—open to *receive* what He wants to give, open to

give back what He wants to take. Acceptance of the will of God means relinquish-
ment of our own will. If our hands are
full of our own plans, we can't
receive His.

Adjustment is a process

The weighty word *adjustment* comes at me from every direction. What does it mean? Acceptance must come first, then adjustment. Lack of acceptance puts up a road block to my healthy adjustment. To adjust means to take something that doesn't fit and do whatever is necessary to make it functional.

My new role as a single again didn't fit me at first. In some ways it was too big, in other ways, too small. I realized that to adjust to my new status, I would need to cooperate with God. Adjustment won't be automatic. I can't heal myself, but I can affect the pace of my healing. I can dig in my heels and delay it. I can also accelerate it.

Adjustment is an ongoing process, and I'll never *arrive.* Learning to be single again isn't an overnight process. As new situations come up, they require new adjustments, an alteration here and there. The Lord and I will be working together to make my new role fit, so I can move on and live to please Him.

The goal of my adjustment is to emerge
into *my own personhood in Christ.*

> I don't think that God expects me to
> adjust permanently to *the transition
> period of widowhood.*

If I can grasp that, I'll gain a new perspective on the road of life ahead. I shouldn't get stuck wearing a sandwich board labeled "widow" for the rest of my life. I may be *single* from now on, but I shouldn't dwell on the fact that I'm a *widow.* A fine line but an important one separates those two views.

How a singled out woman grieves, for how long, and how well she adjusts are partly conditioned by her personality and temperament. No two people have the same responses to trauma. The woman who is accustomed to accept all things as good from the hand of God usually meets life head on as it comes. She understands that life isn't fair and trouble is common to humankind. She'll usually come through any storm of life by trusting in God.

The nervous, high strung, emotional-by-nature woman with a lifelong tendency to anxiety typically takes her loss harder. The one doesn't love more than the other or feel the pain less. A recently singled out friend observed:

> Some women cry about a lot of things. Some women just don't. Some never want to be alone and seek constant company. Some always look for coddling, while others are pretty independent. Some are shy, others wear their hearts on their sleeves. Some will read a book

on bereavement and feel almost guilty because they haven't experienced all the steps of grief. God gives them peace as they trust Him, a peace that may baffle others. The Lord understands our individual reactions because He created us with different temperaments.

Despite our natural diversity, God can redirect our emotional expressions as we look to Him. We can be peaceful, steadfast and unmovable even if nature has inclined us to be shattered by traumas of life. God can help us prevail over our natural reactions when we acknowledge His Lordship.

I'm sure I'll continue to have emotional adjustments, but I'm counting on the Lord to make the rough places smoother. For the rugged places that remain, God will provide sturdy, cushioned hiking boots. For what I don't see around the corner, God will give me grace to trust Him.

All the above and other unlabeled stages, universal grief feelings or whatever we want to call them, are part of the normal grieving process. I can't believe that I was so naive as to think I could suppress and disregard them all. I thought if I could just move quickly past them with blinders on, they wouldn't reach out and grab me and demand my time and effort to deal with them. I found there was no other way than to back up and chug through each of them before I could really move forward to God's fullest and best for the remaining days of my life.

God doesn't expect us to tackle all the universal grief feelings at once or alone. The Lord promised to be with us, gave His Spirit to live in us to guide us into all truth. He is our Comforter, consoling Refuge and strong *Fort*—the secondary meaning of Com*FORT*er.

I struggled with the "firsts" of everything I now had to do alone. Some of them seemed so trivial: The first time I went shopping and stopped for a burger at Ted's favorite fast food place— and sat in "our" booth alone. The first time I went to church alone. I couldn't bring myself to sit in our usual place, so I chose a pew on the opposite side.

A friend wrote me, "The firsts are difficult but bearable, if we don't focus on our loss. Recall and smile at all the great times you had together."

 4 $\quad$ *Making it Through Those "Firsts"*

$\mathcal{T}$he first Thanksgiving gathering, the family Christmas celebration, New Year's eve alone— so many holidays crowded into the first extended month after my husband died—bad calendar timing!

The first time our car wouldn't start, the first time I had to lift something heavy without Ted's help, the first time I rearranged furniture, (my favorite pastime about which he always groaned) the first time seed catalogs arrived in our rural mailbox. The first time official mail arrived for him, and I had to write "deceased" on the envelope.

The first time I was invited to dinner with two other couples, and I sat in the odd chair—a fifth wheel. The first time I answered the phone to a caller who asked to speak to my husband, and I had to tell him Ted had died. The first time I had to balance my checkbook. The first time I had to file tax forms. The first time his favorite magazines arrived.

The first planting season when the garden needed digging. The first time his favorite TV show came on. The first time I got sick, and he wasn't there to brew his special hot herb tea which he always claimed would "cure me fast."

Jesus is my *Alpha*. He is my *First*. As I put Him first, He is able to help me through the struggles of all the "firsts" still ahead.

The first storm

I hurried from my car to the back door with my groceries. Big drops of rain pelted the brown paper bags and my jacket.

Safely in, the groceries quickly stored, I noted anxiously that electric lights were flickering from lightning strikes. Thunder rumbled and clapped too near for comfort. I was alone in a storm for the first time since Ted left for heaven. The sky darkened to an eerie twilight although it was only mid-afternoon. I suddenly felt chilled and very much alone.

I don't usually mind storms. I find the steady rain on the roof without all the thunder and "fireworks" soothing even in the middle of the night. When Ted was here, we would always divide the task and run in different directions shutting windows. When the house was secure, he would settle in his favorite chair and calmly read a book or magazine. Even if I had work elsewhere in the house, I would stay near him, just comforted by his presence. Till the storm passed by.

Now I was alone.

Lightning flashed and thunder crashed. I closed all the windows by myself, even the bedroom window that always stuck, the one my husband took care of. Panic fluttered in the pit of my stomach. I looked around for a comforting place. I settled down in Ted's favorite chair to wait out the storm. His reading glasses were still on the end table along with his books and magazines.

Before long, the sun came out, the air smelled clean and fresh and birds started singing again. I learned later that a tornado had touched down in our area, trees were toppled, hail fell and the wind and rain had been ferocious.

I, too, have been through a sudden emotional storm with the death of my husband. I feel battered. The sun is not yet fully shining, but God has promised to bring me through.

Storm

Fierce, driving rain
lashing my window pane
slashing at house and tree
frightening me with thunder
and flashes, fanfare of power
awesome to see.

Then sudden peace. Torrents cease
rumble is distant, maelstrom muffled
whispering breeze calms my world
a hawk circles silently in slow motion
Robins chirp carefree joy
to the rhythmic accompaniment
of the dripping downspout.

My inward storm, too, is not
a destructive holocaust.
It is Your drama, Lord
Your grand production staged
to teach me Your perfect ways.

Nature's storm is over
and so is mine. Time for applause
time to open the window
breathe the bracing freshness
time to lift my face and revel

in lingering raindrops caressing
my cheek, washing my tears.

Yes, it's time to remember
Your tender mercies, Lord
Your unfailing love
as sun breaks forth
warming my inner chill
and a rainbow crescents
the indigo sky anchoring to a hill
on the horizon, while I worship You, Lord
for Your majestic display
in Your created world and intimately
in the deep recesses of my heart.[1]

I turned on the radio to get a weather report, and a Christian gospel group was singing, "Roses will bloom again, just wait and see. I don't know how or when, but roses will bloom again."

I stepped out on the deck. The sun was shining although a gentle, misty rain was still falling. Suddenly I saw a miniature, yet perfect rainbow low among the trees—not up in the sky! The sun filtered through the leaves of the trees to create the rainbow, and both ends were anchored only a few yards from each other. There it was—*just for me!* No one else in the world could see this small display of promise from God! I focused on it with tear-filled eyes. Within a few minutes it disappeared as clouds floated across the sun.

I accepted it as a sweet, loving reminder from the Lord that He would care for me, He would watch over me, come what may. And His promises would never fail me.

The first Thanksgiving

How could life go on so normally when I'm going through such a painful loss? Somehow I expected all ordinary activity to stop. Another singled out woman expressed, "I looked out the window and wanted to shout at all my neighbors, "How can you act as though nothing has happened? Don't you know my husband died?"

Thanksgiving came the same month Ted died. Less than three weeks later, in fact. We had been living with our eldest son, Rick, while he was building a chalet in the woods for us on his property next door. In earlier years we had hosted our four sons and families for a big bash on Thanksgiving, but in recent years we had been gathering at son Cliff's home, more accessible to our extended family. The same plan was scheduled this time. Rick, however, wouldn't be able to go because, as manager of his radio station, he let his staff take the holiday.

Realizing it would be Rick's first Thanksgiving without his Dad, and I would have to be away for the family celebration the following day, I decided to cook a complete Thanksgiving dinner just for the two of us— baked turkey breast and all the trimmings, candles, tablecloth and decorations. Even my traditional celery and onion dressing which I would make for the family gathering the next day. I made sure we had plenty of cranberry sauce without which Rick maintained turkey could not be eaten.

I must still have been in the numb-shock mode and functioning on automatic pilot. In retrospect, I don't know how I got through such an emotional ordeal, but I felt an inner compulsion to carry on the tradition for our son. I felt Ted would be pleased.

The first Christmas

A month later, just before our annual family Christmas gathering, I spent several long evenings putting together a "This Is Your Life, Ted" in a large loose leaf photo album in memory of him. I sorted through boxes of family photos, (which I should have put into albums years ago) and selected representative photos from all periods of his life starting with his childhood. School days, youth, college, seminary and military service were included. Then our wedding, Ted with our children at various growing stages, then with grandchildren. Many photos were from our ministry and missionary travels together, right up to the last photo taken the day before he died while fishing at Rick's pond. I didn't realize what an emotional project I had attempted, but I'm glad I did it. I may never have done it, if not then. It helped *me* to grasp the reality of his rich life and now of that life's termination.

Our sons and family members each spent time on Christmas day looking through it. Hopefully it also helped them come to terms with the fact that dad and grandpa was no longer with us. The book was a worthy celebration of his life. We laughed together at the good times the photos brought to our memories, while shedding a few tears together and privately.

We celebrated our traditional Christmas at our son Clifford's home an hour and a half drive away. I had gone reluctantly but forced myself because "it was the right thing to do" and I felt obligated to be a strong role model before my family. I had hastily bought gifts and made my traditional dressing to add to the dinner fare.

To tell the truth, I remember little about the occasion. Somehow, finally, it was over. Son Rick and I drove the entire way home in silence, wrapped in our own thoughts and emotions.

The first New Year's Eve

Between the first Christmas and New Year's eve, I was scheduled to participate in a major national Christian convention, *Chinese Mission '92*, where my new book, *Touching China: Close Encounters of the Christian Kind*, was being released. That was the book on which my husband had given me so many constructive suggestions, and which recounted some of the many experiences we had shared in our many trips to China. Ted gave his final approval to the manuscript a few weeks before his death. He took me to our favorite restaurant to celebrate its completion, and joked about helping me autograph the books by imitating my illegible signature.

Day after day I sat at the book signing table and forced myself to socialize with people. Many we had known through our years of ministry, and most hadn't heard that Ted died. Both of us had registered, and Ted eagerly looked forward to fellowship with friends and co-workers. Well-meaning friends kept asking where he was.

I could feel my stress level mounting throughout that week. I was unable to get enough rest because of the packed schedule and one-to-one appointments until late at night. By New Year's eve I was tense from the prolonged social ordeal and exhausted after the long drive home by myself from Washington, D.C. I dreaded that unplanned New Year's eve alone when most people were partying in a festive mood. My raw, suppressed feelings were finally exposed and erupted. I completely lost control emotionally.

Son Rick was also on the ragged edge of exhaustion because of his work at the radio station and still processing his own grief. I can't even remember why, but unexpectedly we argued and shouted unwarranted and unkind words at each other. It was so *un*characteristic of both of us. I can't recall such a thing ever happening before or since. Our family has nearly always been courteous and patient toward one another no matter what our disagreements.

We were both physically spent after the explosion and wounded in our spirits. For the first time since Ted's death I sobbed until I had no more tears left. My stomach was in knots, and my head throbbed with tension. I felt guilty about hurting and offending my son by irresponsibly venting my emotions on him. After a period of sullen silence and inward repentance, we asked forgiveness of each other. We both closed our bedroom doors and went to bed before the whistles and bells heralded the New Year.

I wasn't even spiritually healthy enough
to pray the New Year in.
Surely God understood.

It would be the first New Year without Ted since we were college classmates. I couldn't imagine what the next year would bring or how I would survive even the next month as a new widow. A totally uncharted path lay ahead. My mind felt wiped out, my emotions were on edge and bleeding. I found another reservoir of tears which I dumped into my pillow to welcome the New Year.

Feelings of abandonment

I guess I have a "fix it" fixation. Unfixed trivial things frustrate me all out of proportion to their importance. Unfinished things shout at me. Undone odds and ends undo me. I was blessed and spoiled by having a handyman husband. His skill was not acquired by training—it was a natural ability to figure anything out, improvise if necessary or buy the proper *thing-a-ma-jig* to repair something. By contrast, I'm all thumbs.

I bought a brass clothes tree which came in a big, long cardboard box. When the bolts, screws and sections spilled out on my kitchen floor along with a sheaf of small print instructions, I wanted to cry.

I panicked when I attempted to assemble a simple, wooden drying rack for the laundry room. Hanging curtain rods, pictures, attending to leaky faucets and sundry household breakdowns were major frustrations. Carrying heavy groceries, bringing in logs for the wood stove, starting the fire from scratch on cold mornings and necessary outdoor work left me disheartened. Even a simple bird feeder came with a packet of nuts and bolts and instructions for assembly, so it remained in the box for a month until one of our sons put it together in a minute.

I felt abandoned. I knew my husband didn't die on purpose. I'm sure he would have liked to live longer. Now, having tasted the glories of heaven, I doubt if he would be willing to return and help me with those temporal, mundane things. I can't imagine anything breaking down in heaven—otherwise Ted would have his work cut out for him.

Grief rears its troubling head again. Not grieving for my husband—*grieving and self-pity for me!* I must learn to live in an unfinished, unfixed, imperfect environment. Either I'll have to start fixing things myself or learn patience as I wait for someone to rescue me.

What does the Bible say about acquiring patience? "Tribulation works patience." I can't classify these minor frustrations as tribulations, but I desperately need God's patience to struggle through them.

My husband's personal effects

Some grief counselors recommend that we dispose of our husband's clothing and personal effects within a few months or less. Some suggest that the more personal reminders of our husband we have around the house the more prolonged our grieving process is likely to be. That is not always the case. It is still an individual matter.

Seeing our husband's personal effects around the house all the time may be a constant reminder of our loss, and generally a hindrance to our healthy need to move on with our new lives. We must accept once for all that he will not return to wear them and use them. His present wardrobe in heaven is more glorious than we can imagine. We are advised that it isn't disloyal to begin to move on with our own lives as singled out women.

We could invite our children and other relatives and friends to select what they wish as remembrances. The remainder might be donated to charitable organizations, missions or the like.

Some women go to the opposite and usually unhealthy extreme by keeping their husband's room, closet, workshop, office or garage exactly as he left it without touching a thing. It may be a form of denial and inability to accept the fact that one's husband will not return. We shouldn't judge one another in these matters, however. Emotions are unpredictable in the early months of our grief. We need to take our time to work through such personal decisions.

I had to follow my own way to deal with Ted's possessions. Of course I wanted to keep many things of a private nature and legal or official items of significance such as diplomas, awards, photos, genealogy, historical documents, etc.

I framed several of my husband's pictures and continue to display them prominently around the house where I see them constantly. I want our children and grandchildren and visiting friends to see them and continue to remember their relationship with him. I made a list of his possessions I decided to keep, and designated who is to have them after I leave for heaven.

Everything earthly perishes. Only the spiritual, the unseen is eternal. When I buy a major appliance or some other piece of durable goods now, the thought often flashes before me, "This will probably outlast me." I think of the clothing and possessions of my husband that I have just given away. My husband and I purchased some of them together. They remind me so much of him and his preferences. Some were still new and never worn, like the new jeans for his anticipated fall garden cleanup.

When he bought them, did the thought ever cross his mind that he might never wear them? Did he have any premonition of his soon flight from this world?

My husband was preparing to leave on the next day's flight for an eagerly anticipated visit with his brother and sisters on the West Coast. He had packed several pairs of new socks, underwear and a new sport shirt in his open suitcase. He left for heaven without them. He wouldn't need them. He was immediately clothed with immortality—and whatever they wear in heaven. Since his retirement, he wasn't keen on wearing suits and ties. Maybe there isn't a dress code on downtown Celestial City streets.

As I step through this new door of my life, I'm much more conscious of the implications of Jesus' words:

> Do not be anxious then, saying, 'What shall we eat?' or 'What shall we drink?' or 'With what shall we clothe ourselves?' For all these things the Gentiles eagerly seek; for your heavenly Father knows that you need all these things.
>
> But seek first His kingdom and His righteousness; and all these things shall be added to you. Therefore do not be anxious for tomorrow; for tomorrow will care for itself. Each day has enough trouble of its own. (Matthew 6:31-34).

I come to the garden alone

The first spring arrived. Snow turned into slush, rains came, grass turned lush green again. The robins called me outdoors. In a weak winter moment when seed catalogs jammed our mailbox, this non-gardener ordered a few plants and seed packets. When they were delivered, I was forced to plant them.

For the first time since his death I went into Ted's garden shed for tools. I was overwhelmed with missing him. Yet it was a sweet sadness because I tried to keep remembering that he is enjoying heaven. I wondered what his first Easter in heaven must have been like. Wow!

Because I invaded the earthly venue where my husband "performed" his gardening feats almost daily, my emotions surfaced again. Everything in the garden shed sang of his joy in growing vegetables and fruit. How proudly he brought the products of his labor into our kitchen! We ate our fill of fresh things, shared the abundance with friends and neighbors, and put the surplus in the freezer. My husband bought books on how to make jam and preserve vegetables and fruit. He became expert at dehydrating fruit. It was a new experience for him, and he spent blocks of his retirement time canning (while I "preserved" manuscripts in my computer).

Now his garden lay untilled, unseeded and unweeded. Lacking a green thumb, I never even put gardening on my "to do" list. (My thumbs get their exercise on the space bar of my computer.) Son Rick, on whose property the garden lies, only has time to tend to the fruit trees. I decided to ask the neighbor across the road if he would like to take advantage of our fertile garden soil this year.

The denim cap he always wore to the garden, a Christmas gift from our granddaughters, Kelly and Kara, hung on a nail behind the door. His pith helmet with a solar battery and tiny fan on the crown, given by our sons for his birthday, lay under the workbench covered with cobwebs. Two mismatched left-handed work gloves were stuffed in his dusty work jacket. Mice obviously chewed open many of the seed packets. Ted had been clearing summer brush from the garden and preparing for winter when he got his summons to heaven. His garden rake leaned against the shed outside, undisturbed through the winter snows.

I had suggested to Rick a number of times that we should empty the shed and dispose of rusty tools, out-dated seeds and cob-webby clutter.

The shed with Ted's tools, insecticides,
seeds and garden paraphernalia stood
untouched. As I opened the door with the
rusty hinges, the first thing I saw was his
still mud-caked garden shoes
under the bench.

"No, Mom," he responded, turning away. "Leave the shed alone." I must remember that not only have I lost a husband, but my sons have lost a father. It may be a long time before this son will be ready to do anything about this poignant reminder of his father.

Although I had no experience in gardening, I was motivated by spring air and warm sunshine. I found a few of Ted's basic tools and decided to dig, hoe and sweat preparing a tiny plot near my chalet where I put in the few plants and some seeds. Every muscle in my body ached that night. I wasn't surprised that none of my seeds came up, and the young plants withered and died.

The familiar whir of our neighbor's lawn mower stirred more memories and drew tears. My husband would have had our huge lawn trimmed and manicured at the first hint of spring.

How Ted would have enjoyed this season! The eight young fruit trees he planted as "infants" are now adolescent trees blossoming in the warm sun. His asparagus came up automatically. I wondered about his prized strawberry patch. Would it produce in spite of neglect? His grape arbor sprouted green leaves without any human attention. . . .

I wondered if God assigned Ted to a gardening task in heaven. I wouldn't be surprised. Perhaps he is like Adam, the first man. "The Lord God took the man and put him into the garden of Eden to cultivate it and keep it" (Genesis 2:15). Surely we'll have lots of surprises when we get *There,* the place Jesus said He was preparing for us. He called it "My Father's House." I'm sure Ted already feels at home.

For Ted's memorial service I adapted a poem imagining my husband's new life in heaven.

Letter From Glory

Would you like to know where I am now?
At Home in my Father's House,
in the mansion Jesus prepared for me.
I am where I longed to be
no longer on the stormy sea
but in a safe and quiet harbor.
Death lost its sting; my spirit soared away

incorruptibility replaced mortality.
I'm perfect now in holiness,
no stumbling, bumbling ways.
Working time is done and I am resting.
Sowing time is over and with joy
I reap the harvest!

Do you want to know what it's like here?
The blind see God face to face
not through a glass darkly
the sight is awesome!
Gardens and fruit trees are magnificent
and fishing is exciting in the crystal sea!

Guess what I'm doing?
Singing hallelujahs with angel choirs
to Him who sits on the throne.
Now I have those "thousand tongues" I longed for
to sing my Great Redeemer's praise.

Do you know who else is here?
A blessed company
better than the best reunion on earth:
saints from ages past
loved ones and friends,
and those with whom I served the Lord.
We're celebrating new arrivals all the time.

Do you know how long this will last?
Forever, imagine!
Heaven's food is terrific
and I don't get drowsy after lunch.
Everything here is as new as when God created it.

This is the Eternity we talked about together!

Therefore, don't weep for *me*. Just be sure
you, too, will be in this Triumphant Company
the Church blood-bought by Christ on Calvary!

Excuse me, I have to go—
we're having a Family reunion.
I can't believe I'm meeting Abraham,
King David, and the Apostle Paul! [2]

Jennie, a singled out friend, wrote me of her gardening experience. Her missionary husband also loved gardening.

I wonder what you and I are going to do in heaven while both of our husbands are working God's gardens. A neighbor plowed Tom's garden the first year after his death "in memory of your husband," he said. Another neighbor remarked, "I saw you working in *your husband's* garden." He spoke in a *how dare you?* accusing tone, as if I were desecrating my husband's property.

That is what I ask myself—*how dare I?* I planted bulbs that never came up, beans that never sprouted and even messed up on cucumbers and squash. I sobbed, "Oh, Tom, I hope you are *not* watching this!"

Sarah, also singled out, wrote of how her husband Joel's love for gardening was commemorated.

Joel was a great gardener, always raising more vegetables than we could possibly use, but he never sold them—he gave them away. As a fitting setting for his memorial service, a friend made an arrangement of vegetables from our garden for the worship center. Potatoes, onions, squash, tomatoes, beets, turnips, carrots and celery—all grown from seeds Joel had planted. Those were given away to friends who came to the service.

One of the last things Joel did in his garden was to pick up walnuts from our English walnut tree in our yard. Those we placed in baskets at the exits of the church, and the pastor invited everyone to take a walnut home and plant it in Joel's memory. Truly an uplifting memorial following his six months of suffering.

The one-year fence

Most of us have heard that a singled out woman should not make major decisions for at least one year. Some quickly sell their home, move into an apartment or change location. Others change their occupation or go immediately to work. Or retire from work. Psychologists tell us that only one drastic change per year can bring on trauma—the death of a spouse is *already one change* and enough to cope with.

As I compare notes with my singled out friends, I realize that sometimes it's not advisable or impossible to wait a year before making some of those changes. Finances may be a consideration. At best, moving causes physical, emotional and mental stress. It helps if the move is a happy, anticipated and voluntary one, but that's not always the case. Failing health or strength may enter the picture.

If we can coast awhile without making major adjustments, we would do better. But if major changes are absolutely necessary, we should trust the care and guidance of our Lord. Impulsive decisions that thrust us into an unfamiliar situation are the kind we may later regret. We should listen to the counsel of our family and concerned friends whom we trust, but having done so, we should evaluate their advice and ask the Lord for clear guidance.

A major milestone

Friends advised me to plan for the first anniversary of Ted's death. As the day drew near, I struggled between ignoring the occasion and going on with life as I was now living it, or making some kind of landmark experience out of it. I wanted to be sensitive to the needs of our children and grandchildren who had lost their father and grandfather. I knew there would be phone calls and notes from family and close friends.

Some expected me to be emotional about the day, especially those who had been through the experience. They were prepared to comfort me and offered many suggestions.

I needed to do whatever was best for me. I let my family know my needs and asked for their support and understanding. I wanted some extended time alone and time with family.

I didn't even get to say goodbye because I didn't know he was leaving. Neither did he. I needed some way to mark the emotional completion of a relationship that had, in fact, ended. But in my mind it still dangled with loose ends.

As I considered my own needs, I realized that because my husband died so suddenly, I had *an unfinished feeling.* I know that in God's sovereign plan He didn't cut short Ted's life before his course was finished. But *it is I* who have unfinished business.

I decided to write a letter to my husband on the anniversary of his departure. I couldn't mail it to heaven, of course, and he wouldn't receive it. No one else would ever see the letter because I would destroy it.

It seemed like a good idea. I needed to tell him how I was doing after a year had passed, even though he is in Eternity where time is not counted. A tangible letter would give me some sense of closure. Then I could let go and say a final goodbye. I did just that.

I wrote to tell him how my heart ached because I was not with him when the Lord called him Home. I asked him what it was like to die and whether he suffered. Was he surprised to wake up in heaven instead of in his own bed? I asked him whether he knew about the memorial services and the wonderful tributes of his family, friends and co-workers.

I asked if heaven was like we speculated
when we used to talk about it. I inquired
by name whether certain family members
and friends were there, and whether he
had any surprises in that respect.

Had he already met friends who arrived in heaven
during the year since he left? I asked how he could
recognize people without their bodies. I told him news
about each of our sons—Rick, Cliff, Gary and Jeff, their
families and their careers. And how each was always
ready to help me—filing my income tax, pooling resources to upgrade my car to a newer model, giving me
counsel on finances, including me in their plans, inviting
me to spend time in their homes, remembering special
days with gifts and visits, taking me out for meals, fixing
things around my chalet, solving my computer problems,
and phoning me often to check on my welfare. I told him
how proud he would be of them.

I described how grown up all the grandchildren
were and something about their school achievements. I
reported about the ministries we shared and the Christian radio station we helped establish. I told him about
the national and world situation and how the election
came out after he left. And all about the new church
where I'm worshiping and new friends I've made.

I told him about his garden and fruit trees, how his
relatives were doing and how I'm adjusting to my living-
alone role. I shared a few jokes with him about how

frustrated I feel without him when things around the house go wrong—and how Rick always rallies to help.

I informed him on the progress of my new book manuscripts and the exciting ideas I'm working on, and about my trip overseas and news of people we had met when we traveled there together. About our family plans for the upcoming holidays, the beauty of the first November snowfall and the feathery flutter around my new bird feeders.

I told him how snug I felt when I wore the fuzzy, warm blue robe he bought me in advance for Christmas last year—not imagining he wouldn't be on earth for Christmas. I told him I was using the touch-on lamp by my bedside that I bought him as an advance gift for Christmas, and which he used for only a few weeks before his death.

I asked what Christmas was like in heaven. Did the angels sing an encore of their performance above Bethlehem the night Christ was born? And how did they celebrate Easter in heaven? Did people there know what's happening on earth?

Then I told him I would always love him.

And I told him goodbye.

Second anniversary

Time passes so quickly. The day before the second anniversary of his death, I pulled on my hiking boots, zipped up my winter jacket and stuffed my ski cap in my pocket against the unseasonable chill. With Ted's woods-walking stick I set off for a trek through the woodland surrounding the chalet we had designed together.

I relived the day before his death. It had been a warm autumn day in November. We didn't even need coats for church. Ted drove us to one of his favorite restaurants after church, and he ate heartily, remarking with a laugh, "I've eaten so much you won't need to make supper tonight!" Upon returning home, we changed clothes and hiked the woodland where I was retracing our steps.

I had taken a camera along and asked him to pose by the lake with his fishing pole which he was putting away for the winter. That snapshot is framed on a shelf above my computer hutch. We kicked the colorful fallen leaves and chased squirrels. I continued hiking while Ted returned to the chalet to make a bonfire where he spent several hours until early dusk burning building debris and branches to clear the driveway access to our partly finished chalet.

Today I kicked leaves alone, watched scampering squirrels alone, then sat in the same but considerably rustier lawn chair where I snapped Ted's picture two years before. Canadian geese honked in flight overhead, a frog splashed from the bank through the reeds at the pond's edge. Life goes on.

Falling Leaf

In the season of
the falling leaf
my falling tears
splash hot
upon my pillow
in the dark night
of my quiet grief
for what might have been
but can be no more.
I bow to God's decrees.

Nevertheless. . .
I can't suppress
my lonely tears
flowing silently
from a heart severed
from my love
like the autumn leaf
turned brown
detached from tree-life
floats without sound
to the ground.[3]

On the actual day of the second anniversary of Ted's death I decided I might finally be able to deal with four remaining boxes of sundries from his bedroom that I had stashed in a closet.

For a long time I had tried to get Ted to sort those accumulated odds and ends himself. He was always reluctant to decide what to toss or what to keep when it came to obsolete things. He had a squirrel tendency to keep everything "in case I might need it sometime." Now I was left with the job.

Six pairs of old eyeglasses, five watches with broken crystals or missing stems—one still running on its battery although time had stopped for its owner. Rubber bands around scores of business cards from acquaintances all over the world, old photos, used travel tickets and an antiquated blood pressure kit. Shaving kits with rusty razors, glue tubes, two dozen empty plastic prescription containers. A 35-mm camera he had used on many overseas ministry trips, a box of coins from other countries, three expired passports and one still valid. Old calendars, six year's worth of checking account stubs, his worn personal Bible and daily devotional journal in his familiar handwriting. And much more miscellanies.

As I handled each item, memories overwhelmed me. Yes, it was time to sort, toss, and keep. I put the keepsakes in a box which already held the video tape and audio tape of Ted's memorial services made by his nephew (which I haven't had the courage to view again). The box also contained newspaper clippings of his death, tributes by friends and co-workers, the visitors' book and a list of sympathy cards and letters received.

I sealed the box, brewed a cup of Ted's favorite Jasmine tea, and sat in his re-cliner gazing out the window through tear-blurred eyes until dusk.

The softly falling rain beat a tattoo against the window pane as a brisk wind shook the remaining leaves from November branches. I watched the rain turn into swirling snow and recalled how one week after his death as the family drove to Washington, D.C. for Ted's second memorial service, a sudden blizzard whipped up. We could hardly see a car-length ahead as the fierce wind blew big white flakes almost horizontally toward us. The early onset of cold weather seemed symbolc of my loss.

I reminisced about events following his death. All four of our sons stayed with me the entire week. On impulse I asked them to clear out and clean their father's bedroom. I knew I would never be able to attempt such an emotional task in the near future, if they didn't do it for me. I didn't stop to consider how difficult a request I was making. I only thought about sparing myself. They didn't refuse me, and silently set to the task. They stripped the bed, did the laundry, emptied the closet of their father's clothes, packed them in boxes, and put the personal effects of his desk and contents of bureau drawers in the boxes I had just dealt with.

I asked each son to take anything he wished in remembrance of his father. I can't even recall what they took.

Why did I feel such an urgency to do that? Perhaps I had a flashback to my early teen years when my live-in grandmother died. In the days between her death and the funeral, my parents did the same thing with her personal effects. I watched in numb and wide-eyed silence. Obviously, that was what should be done. Our family was programmed to accept the inevitable without undue emotion and move on quickly. Perhaps we needed the safety zone of normal activities in the company of family members so we wouldn't think about our human loss. I subconsciously imitated that mindset during the immediate events that followed Ted's death.

During the memorial service, Kelly, my eldest teen granddaughter, left her place beside her mother and slid into the pew beside me. Her freely flowing tears stained my jacket and blouse. I gladly held her close mingling my own tears with hers. But by the time of the reception afterward, I regained control of my emotions and kept them in check to greet friends, carry on everyday conversations and be the role model everyone expected.

> I can't believe I calmly greeted people at
> the door of the church before the memo-
> rial services. I remained mostly tearless,
> reminding others with a smile that this
> gathering was a celebration for Ted.

On the second anniversary of Ted's death, I rummaged in the storage area for a slab of birch wood with an
oil painting of a sea gull winging into the sky—alone. My
son, Clifford, bought it for me while he was on vacation
at the beach some years before. I pounded a nail in the
wall and hung it in my dining area. To me it symbolized
moving on, soaring into the unknown as a single again—
but with God.

I bought a cello-pack of walnuts at the Safeway
market where Ted and I used to shop. I put them in a
decorative basket on the coffee table. I don't eat walnuts,
but Ted was fond of them. He always bought a package
in November to crack and munch on through the holidays, especially while watching TV. Ted died in early
November before he had a chance to eat any. That first
Thanksgiving I gave the basket of nuts and his gold-
plated nut cracker to my son, Clifford, when we gathered
at his home for the first festivities without Ted.

I don't eat cornflakes. I prefer other varieties of
cereal. Ted ate nothing but cornflakes for breakfast all
the years of our marriage! I bought a box of Kellogg's
cornflakes at the same time I purchased the walnuts. Ted
sometimes bought generic products but refused to com-

promise on cornflakes. The morning of November 9, two years after his death, I ate a bowl of cornflakes with a sliced banana—as he always did. I toasted a piece of his favorite rye bread and spread it with strawberry jam which Ted himself preserved from his strawberry patch the summer before he died. I sipped Jasmine tea made from tea leaves we bought together in Beijing, China. I ate that breakfast with tear-filled eyes. Sweet sadness.

Rick brought me two handsful of the first crop of persimmons from the young tree Ted so proudly planted and nurtured. Out of those I made one small jar of jam in remembrance.

The week before, I had gone to the polling booths at the Gainsboro Fire Station to vote. Another *deja vu* experience. Two years before, Ted and I voted a few days prior to his death. He hurried through breakfast and took along his second cup of tea to finish in the car. He was an informed and responsible citizen, often sending his comments on current issues to the *Readers Opinion* section of the *Winchester Star*. After we voted, he asked for two "I voted" decals, one for his jacket and one for the bumper of our car.

We went shopping afterward for kitchen floor vinyl and carpeting for my new writing studio in the chalet we were building. At noon we headed for hamburgers and free senior citizen coffee at McDonald's. Ted stopped at the counter to sign up for a free breakfast on his birthday in a few months. A week later Ted was in heaven. Now I walk alone on the floor vinyl we picked out. I vacuum the blue sculptured carpet we selected for my studio.

Just before his January birthday I opened our rural mailbox to find a postcard addressed to Ted. "Warmest Birthday Wishes! Bring this card to McDonald's and receive a free *Egg McMuffin* and cup of coffee or tea". A similar postcard arrives each year. I just haven't notified them to cancel it yet.

Almost daily I sit at the new computer hutch Ted assembled in anticipation of moving it to our chalet after it was built. I glance at his smile in one of his photos framed on the wall, interpreting it as approval for the adjustment I've made since he left. Does he know what I'm doing? Or are the glories of heaven so all-consuming that those in the presence of God are not concerned with what is happening on planet Earth?

In fact, I hope he *doesn't* know how frustrated I become still trying to balance my checkbook. Ted always did it for me. In the months that followed, when I utterly failed to balance it—I mean when I'm *way off*—I asked one or another of our sons to rescue me. Eventually I felt I shouldn't bother them anymore in their busy lives. I kept trying to do it myself. Sometimes I succeeded, more often I failed. I finally decided that since I have a small checking account at two banks, I could write checks exclusively on only one for a month or so until it was time for another bank statement. Then I accepted the other bank's balance whether I agreed with it or not and started fresh—until my next mixup.

I can imagine how Ted would chuckle at my childish strategy!

Third anniversary

Winter surprised us early this year. Large, gentle flakes of snow started to descend about mid-afternoon. They fell in slow motion against the somber gray sky and green pines outside my chalet. Soon the gravel driveway, the woodpile on the deck and the bird feeders looked as if white cake flour had been sifted over them.

On the commemorative day of Ted's Homegoing each year, I set aside time from my writing and household doings to reflect on the past and evaluate my ongoing single life. I put normal activities on hold and I, too, yield to slow motion. I pulled my recliner closer to the wood stove and allowed memories to trickle into my spirit. Can it be that another year has passed?

I watched the handsome cardinal in his pontifical red coat hop in the snow with his modestly garbed mate and carefully select the fat, black sunflower seeds out of the wild birdseed mix. Charlotte, my purry-furry calico indoor cat, crouches in attack posture, tail switching in quiet rhythm, eyes riveted on the entertaining antics of two young squirrels scampering on the deck. Thermopane sliding doors keep the little animals safe and unattainable while giving Charlotte a ringside view. I wouldn't have adopted Charlotte while Ted was living—he was allergic to cats.

I sat alone staring at the winter scene. The outdoor picnic table was already marshmallowed with fresh snow. Ted and I ate our lunch there many times in the

spring and summer during the construction of our chalet
so we could watch the progress of the carpenters.

Then Ted left so suddenly. We didn't plan that, but
God did. He simply didn't tell us in advance. What would
we have done differently had we known? God is merciful
and loving to withhold knowledge of the future.

It was time for my annual anniversary letter to
Ted.

Do you know how I've been doing? Have
you seen my bungling as I've tried to make it on
my own doing the things you always did so
willingly and well? I try to get the fire started
in the wood stove each cold winter morning.
You were so good at it, blowing patiently on the
few, still glowing embers until they began to
flame. I'm tired of carrying firewood in. I don't
think I'll use the wood stove this winter. I'm
going to depend on my electric baseboard heat-
ing no matter how expensive it is. I'll economize
somewhere else. I'm not eager to compete with
my pioneer ancestors.

Do you see the unfinished odds and ends
around the house that still bug me? The shelves
that aren't put up yet in the laundry room, the
storm door that needs to be put on, the screen
that needs mending? The halogen lamp needs
rewiring and one flood light bulb outdoors has
burned out.

Have you seen my struggles to make this
a home without you? We planned to enjoy these
winter days together in comfortable companionship recalling our worldwide travel ministry and working on our photo albums. We were

dreaming of future adventures as a couple. I feel so alone today. It doesn't seem to get any easier. I love you and miss you. It's almost dark but it's only 4:30. The snow is piling up. Tomorrow I must shovel a path to the car with the snow shovel you bought the week before you left. I kept your brown leather winter gloves for driving. I think of you every time I wear them.

Remember how we pored over designs of our chalet together? We adjusted the size of rooms to suit activities we'd carry on in each area, planning for your special reading and TV nook and my writing studio. I remember how you altered the plans at the last minute to include a hall. I don't know what I'd do without it now. We planned a spacious kitchen because we were going to try many new Chinese recipes at our leisure and change our routine to eat our main meal at noon. We designed the big picture window panels where we could watch every season's spectacular display. We measured with a yard stick the placement of our furniture, bookcases and beds.

We never got to live here together. In the months after your death, I wanted Rick to hurry and finish the chalet so I could move in. I grew impatient with the unavoidable delay caused by snow and ice storms.

Rick accomplished building and decorating miracles in spite of his busy schedule and the adverse weather. Months later I moved in without you. Friends said it was too bad that we didn't get to move in together, but I now see God's hand in the timing. It is better this way, without all the poignant memories I would have if we moved in just before you died.

Cleaning the basement alone

Eventually we must start doing things our husbands usually did or whatever was left undone when they departed for heaven.

When I thought about cleaning the major storage areas—basement, workshop, garage, garden sheds and closet shelves—anger surfaced, self-pity took over, frustration reared its ugly head. All those emotions squeezed in on me when I started on the basement. It wasn't simply a matter of cleaning or rearranging, but serious sorting, disposing of and giving away mountains of accumulation from a lifetime. I had to decide what was useful in my life alone and what was archival stuff or historically significant to me or my posterity. The latter I needed to identify, label and repack.

I confess that I resented having to do this alone instead of with Ted, who liked to put off such chores. My sons were ready to help, and I appreciated their help, but I had to make the final decisions on what to do with stuff. If not I, who? If not now, when?

Cliff helped me in the sorting and hauling, and Rick dug two giant pits with his backhoe at the lower end of his country property. Into one pit we planned to throw non-biodegradables that we hoped no one would ever see again. Perhaps a future generation might unearth them in an archaeological dig and speculate what use they might have had in our period of history. Into the second pit we tossed burnables.

Going through boxes of photos and mementos from our past years of marriage and ministry opened fresh memories. The chore exposed me again to both the near and distant past. I took several steps backward from the adjustment I thought I was making. I was closing the book on large chunks of our life together.

I sensed that if I didn't accomplish this difficult task, I'd be leaving it for my family to do after I left for heaven. They wouldn't have the slightest idea of either the significance or triviality of those material things. I did it partly to relieve their future burdens, partly for my sake. I needed to bury the past. It was part of "setting my house in order."

I came away with new convictions. I'm determined to travel light for the rest of my life journey. I will appreciate and enjoy material things—*if they belong to someone else*. I'll carefully decide what is of value to my life *as it is now*, and what I need for carrying out the Lord's new assignment. I won't covet more or better or bigger or newer things. I will throw the ballast overboard to lighten my life ship.

Always more "firsts"

During several years following my husband's death, I thought surely I had exhausted all the "firsts" with which I would have to struggle. Wrong. "Firsts" of other kinds continue to appear on my adjustment path—some I never dreamed of. As I face into the wind and lean on the Lord, I know He will be with me to help me work through other "firsts" yet to come. "Jesus Christ is the same yesterday and today, yes and forever" (Hebrews 13:8). 🐾

I personally believe that to be reminded of biblical truths during the time of bereavement is a realistic, God-given coping mechanism, not a copout. It isn't wishful thinking, sugary sentiment or a cover up. I desperately needed such theological affirmation.

5 *Checking My Scriptural Anchors*

"Forget your Bible verses," some professional grief counselors advise. "They go right over the heads of the bereaved or may upset them."

People disagree about the wisdom of reminding the Christian widow or widower too soon about the biblical assurances surrounding the death of a Christian spouse. One reason given for not doing so is that the grieving spouse just doesn't want to hear them.

All of us respond to loss by death in different ways. In my own experience, from the moment I realized my husband's spirit left his body, I eagerly and deliberately tried to focus my thoughts on the truth that he was already in the presence of the Lord he loved. That was my bedrock comfort. Every reminder of that from family, friends, by phone calls and sympathy cards built up my faith. Through the traumatic hours that followed, the emotionally-charged memorial services and all the decisions that could have overwhelmed me, I was nourished and sustained by promises from God's Word. I certainly didn't fake that comfort.

Most of my singled out Christian friends feel likewise, but I must recognize that some of them don't, and I must respect their feelings. To Ted and me eternal life was the cornerstone of our Christian lives during 45 years of marriage. It was the message we shared with others during our lifetime of ministry. Preparation for eternity is what the Christian life is all about.

Within a few days after my husband's death a friend sent me an album of cassette tapes about heaven. The messages were soundly Scriptural. I was eager to review what I already knew about life beyond life and add to my knowledge. I now had a vested interest in the topic: Ted was already experiencing heaven! As a Christian wife, I wanted to be reminded that my husband was rejoicing in God's presence with no more pain, tears or trials. That reassured and excited me.

We have a biblical basis for encouraging one another with the Scriptures. Paul counseled believers who were anxious about the state of their recent Christian dead, "Therefore comfort one another *with these words*" (1 Thessalonians 4:18). What words? That our loved ones are with Jesus now, (v. 14) and they will come back to earth with Him when He returns for His Church. If we are still alive at that time, their bodies will rise to meet Him before we do. We'll be caught up with them in the clouds to meet the Lord in the air. Then we will always be with the Lord. We believe this, the apostle said, because of Jesus' own death and resurrection.

It is *this news* that is intended to give us comfort and is to be the substance of what we share with each other in the face of death.

Nevertheless, let's not judge or criticize each other for our reactions in the early hours, days and weeks after the death of our spouses. Let's be especially sensitive, patient, loving, caring and understanding.

The Holy Spirit whom Jesus called *The Comforter*

is the One who knows best how to apply His healing balm to the brokenhearted. He will comfort us and teach us how to sensitively comfort our singled out friends.

The Finish Line

I have met death face to face. My emotions are still tender. They probably will be for a long time. But let's look at death once more, perhaps from a little distance, to see things more realistically and biblically.

Some of us may want to back off and not look at death again so soon, but I think it will be spiritually health-giving and assuring. "Even though I walk through the valley of the shadow of death, I will fear no evil, for you are with me; your rod and your staff, they comfort me" (Psalm 23:4). Look carefully at the term "the valley of *the shadow of death.*" Someone said, "Death can only throw its *shadow* across the valley. Shadows never hurt anyone."

Why shouldn't we fear evil? Because of the presence of God. "For You are with me." God's rod and staff are my comfort.

Let's do a quiet walk-through together—*you and I with God.*

First, a look at our earthly bodies. They are only perishable containers. Second Corinthians chapters four and five point out clearly that we human beings are fragile, earthen vessels. Simply clay pots for temporary use. Good news or bad?

For the Christian it's good news because God had a perfect reason for creating you and me in such fragile containers: so that "everyone can see that the glorious power within must be from God and is not our own" (2 Corinthians 4:7 TLB). When I'm able to live victoriously in this transient body, all the credit must go to God.

Paul said "our outer nature is wasting away." Other versions translate that phrase, "our bodies are dying," "our outer nature suffers decay," "our outward man perishes." Our visits to the dentist, doctor, chiropractor and beauty salon underscore that prognosis. As a Christian, I recognize that *my body is only a tent,* a temporary shelter for my use on this planet. That is, until we occupy them again at the resurrection. Even if I take medications or have surgeries, they are only maintenance procedures.

At my birth, deterioration began to set in and my human body clock started ticking toward a countdown. Early in life, we're told, our brain cells begin to diminish. Happy thought! Sooner than we want to admit, muscle tone and bone structure start downhill.

None of us is created to hang around on planet Earth very long. The good news is what happens to us after our earthly model is "discontinued."

Jesus Christ promised when He left Earth in His resurrected body that He was going to prepare our permanent living quarters elsewhere. Christians are to have a new habitat! Since I belong to Him, I have my reservation there. He promised to exchange my fragile earth-body for *a new model* suited for living in His eternal kingdom.

Therefore, during our lives on earth we should be realistic and expect broken, worn and diseased parts. Medical science races to design "spare parts" for organs that no longer function, but earthly body shop repair has limits. Parts of me will eventually break down, run down and wear out. We can patch some things—fillings for teeth, (or a replacement set) hairpieces, heart bypasses, prosthetic limbs, hip sockets, lens implants and pacemakers. We submit to the removal of lumps and bumps and growths. Illnesses may be slowed for awhile, but some are terminal. Accidents happen as part of earth's free-will-of-man setup. Sooner or later everyone's earthly tent will fold. My life may be extended but only for a while. I can't become an entirely bionic person. No big deal. Our spirit will depart from our clay container.

So what does that mean to me in the loss of my Christian husband?

You and I are not the only ones in the world whose spouses' clay pots broke or wore out, and their earthly tents folded. Death is a common denominator. Of course separation by death hurts terribly. We miss the one we love, one with whom we shared our earthly lives. But life is not over until it's over. For the Christian there is eternity—life will *never* be over!

Rather than dwelling on the question, "Why did he die?" a grief support group decided to focus on asking, "Why did my loved one live?" They found comfort and encouragement by recounting and appreciating the qualities, accomplishments and contributions of the one who died, and how he enriched the lives of family, friends and community.

Birthing into new life

Another way to look at death is birth into new life. Philip Yancey quoted Joseph Bayly as the source of the following analogy:

> Ironically, the one event which probably causes more emotional suffering than any other—death—is in reality a translation, a time for great joy when Christ's victory will be appropriated to each of us. Describing the effect of His own death, Jesus used the simile of a woman in labor, travailing until the moment of childbirth when all is replaced by ecstasy. (John 16:21)

> Each of our deaths can be seen as a birth. Imagine what it would be like if you had full consciousness as a fetus and could now remember those sensations:

> Your world is dark, safe, secure. You are bathed in warm liquid, cushioned from shock. You do nothing for yourself; you are fed automatically, and a murmuring heartbeat assures you that someone larger than you fills all your needs. Your life consists of simple waiting—you're not sure what to wait for, but any change seems far away and scary. You meet no sharp objects, no pain, no threatening adventures. A fine existence.

> One day you feel a tug. The walls are falling in on you! Those soft cushions are now pulsing and beating against you, crushing you downwards. Your body is bent double, your limbs twisted and wrenched. You're falling,

upside down. For the first time in your life, you feel pain. You're in a sea of roiling matter. There is more pressure, almost too intense to bear. Your head is squeezed flat, and you are pushed harder, harder into a dark tunnel. Oh, the pain! Noise! More pressure.

You hurt all over. You hear a groaning sound and an awful, sudden fear rushes in on you. It is happening—your world is collapsing! You're sure it's the end! You see a piercing, blinding light. Cold, rough hands pull at you. A painful slap. Waaaahhhhh!

Congratulations, *you have just been born!* Death is like that. On this end of the birth canal, it seems fiercesome, portentous, and full of pain. Death is a scary tunnel, and we are being sucked toward it by a powerful force. None of us looks forward to it. We're afraid. It's full of pressure, pain, darkness . . . the unknown. But beyond the darkness and the pain *there's a whole new world outside!* When we wake up after death in that bright new world, our tears and hurts will be mere memories. [1]

Yancey comments that although the new world is so much better than this one, we have no vocabulary to accurately describe it. The best the Bible writers can tell us is that we will be in the presence of God and see Him face to face. Our birth into new creatures will be complete.

We shall be changed (transformed). For this perishable [part of us] must put on the imperishable [nature], and this mortal [part of us]—this nature that is capable of dying—

must put on immortality (freedom from death).
And when this perishable puts on the imperishable and this [that was] capable of dying
puts on freedom from death, then shall be
fulfilled the Scripture that says, Death is swallowed up (utterly vanquished, forever) in and
unto victory. O death, where is your victory? O
death, where is your sting? . . . But thanks be to
God, Who gives us the victory—making us
conquerors—through our Lord Jesus Christ. (1
Corinthians 15:52-55,57 The Amplified Bible)

Whatever we may have to go through now is less
than nothing compared with the magnificent future God
has planned for us. The whole creation is on tiptoe to see
the wonderful sight of the sons of God coming into their
own. . . . (Romans 8:18,19 Phillips)

*As much as I enjoy life on planet Earth, Lord, I'm
also on tiptoes of anticipation for that time when I'll be
"coming into my own" in Your presence! Like my husband
has already done!*

Beautiful gateway?

For the Christian, death *is* undeniably the gateway to the next phase of our marvelous eternal life. But,
let's face it, the gateway itself is *not* attractive. We should
not be either maudlin or unrealistic about it. Some of us
singled out women have accompanied our husbands on a
long journey of months, even years, of the painful and
deteriorating process of dying.

"Death is just a normal part of life" is a comment
we often hear, and which Christians are inclined to
accept without examining its *false biblical premise.* Death

is *not* natural. It is always our enemy. We were not born to die. It isn't God's cruel design to make us suffer. Death is not beautiful, no matter how cosmeticized or sentimentalized. Charles Stanley speaks to the point in his book, *How to Handle Adversity*:

> God never intended for man to experience the adversity and sorrow brought about by our forefather's sin. Death was not a part of God's original plan for man. Death is an interruption. It is God's enemy as well as man's. It is the opposite of all He desired to accomplish. Sickness and pain are certainly no friends of God. There was no sickness in the Garden of Eden. The ministry of Christ bears witness to this truth. Everywhere He went He healed the sick. God shares our disdain for disease.
>
> Sickness is an intruder. It had no place in God's world in the beginning; it will have no place in His world in the end. (Revelation 21:3-4) Death, disease, famine, earthquakes, war— these things were not part of God's original plan. Yet they are part of our reality. Why? Did God lose His grip? Has He abandoned us? Is He no longer a good God?
>
> [On the contrary] our reality has been fashioned by Adam's choice to sin. And sin always results in adversity. It is God who will wipe away every tear. It is God who will do away with death, crying, pain, and sorrow.[2]

For the present, human death *still has a sting* to our bodies and minds. Tears and anguish are part of it. It *is* our *enemy*, not our friend. It is not "friendly fire" but the enemy's artillery. Under the best of circumstances it is not pleasant. It is wretched, often painful, prolonged, separating loved ones, sometimes cutting a productive life short. It seems wasteful. We are not realistic if we try to sugarcoat it. The sickness often associated with death may be dreadful.

We must focus our attention on what is *beyond* that gateway. Jesus Christ conquered death by taking that sting upon Himself and leading the way through it by His own agonizing *death and resurrection*.

Separated

I say, "My husband died." But that's not completely true. Only one part of him actually died—his body. That was the temporary part I was so familiar with. The part I recognized, that needed food, got tired and grew older through the years. It had physical limitations and, at times, illnesses.

The part of him that *did not die* was the part *I never saw*. I could only see the expressions of his spirit and soul. The spiritual, eternal, real part of my husband continues to live. That is what left when his body died, and immediately continued living forever in the presence of Christ.

I may find it difficult to think of my husband in two (or three, if you count body, soul, and spirit) parts. But if I can grasp that biblical truth, it helps me understand that my Christian husband is *not dead*. He is living more vitally than he ever lived while joined to his body for so many years.

I should visualize him as alive. That is not the same as unhealthy and unrealistic denial, one of the so-called stages of the grieving process. I accept the fact that his body *is* truly dead. But the *real Ted* is Elsewhere. That transforms my grieving into joy for his sake. The grief I need to deal with is for myself.

He is not still here!

When something happens, whether good, exciting, happy, newsy, or unhappy, troubling or disturbing, my first thought is to share it with Ted. Years and years of this thought pattern color my reactions. Now I get a queasy feeling in the pit of my stomach when I realize he's no longer here to share with me. And never will be.

I have singled out friends who have fallen into the imaginative habit of continuing to talk to their departed spouse as if he were present. Some carry it to the extreme and withdraw into their own world. They leave their husband's room and possessions as they were, as if he were there, as if he were coming back. They say they feel his presence, sense his guidance. Those not grounded in the Word of God may even fall into the subtle occult trap of trying to communicate with the dead.

My husband is really *no longer here.* Nothing in the Bible suggests that spirits of departed ones continue with us. Nothing suggests they can communicate with us. My husband is *Elsewhere.* Whether he even knows what is happening on earth is not certain.

Hebrews 11:16 assures me, "They desire a better country, that is, an heavenly: wherefore God . . . hath prepared for them a city." My husband is literally in another city, in another real place, in a home that Jesus actually prepared for him. Obviously Jesus did not think it was important to go into detail about life in the heavenly realm.

But Jesus did speak of that place in concrete

terms. "In my Father's house there are many dwelling places (homes). If it were not so, I would have told you, for I am going away to prepare a place for you" (John 14:2 Ampl.).

When Jesus was on earth, He wasn't at home. Planet Earth wasn't His realm. He said that He had nowhere to lay His head, no address to permanently reside. He was always on the move in His ministry. Later He would depart for His *real Home,* to the place He enjoyed with His Father from Eternity past.

He must have been aware that "a place" is important to us. He promised that He was going to prepare that place—a nesting, resting place in heaven where we would truly feel "at home." I need to grasp that biblical truth so I won't fall into the error that some books on grief actually advocate:

> Are you seeing "ghosts"? It is common for men and women who have lost their marriage partners to continue to feel, see, even seem to touch their presence for some time after they have died.
>
> Author John Erskine described this special experience. "I know by personal experience that the dead whom we have loved do not leave us, but in some fashion continue here as faithful companions, sustaining and inspiring us. We find them in familiar places, in the home, in the garden, on the street. This constant resurrection of the dead is for me a simple fact, part of my human acquaintance with the daily mystery and beauty of life." [3]

The above is not true. It is biblically false. Such thinking or imagining borders on the occult. *Our Christian loved ones are Elsewhere,* not present with us and guiding us, sustaining us, inspiring us.

This is not the same as easing one's pain like my singled out friend, Gladys, who gained comfort by regularly studying her minister-husband's Bible with its penned marginal notes, and reading it while sitting in his favorite chair. That was healthy and rewarding.

What I *do* need to concentrate on is the truth that *God is here with me.* It is *the Lord* with whom I need to talk, to ask for guidance, spend time with, share things with. Talking aloud to the Lord *is* healthy—that's what prayer is. We communicate with "The Alive" and not the dead. By so doing we cultivate the habit of "praying without ceasing."

Not lost forever

A manual on grief for widows stated, "To be widowed is to suffer one of life's most profound losses. When a loving tie is severed, so is a part of us. What has been lost is lost forever."

A profound loss, yes. The feeling of severance and separation is a deeply felt fact. But for the Christian singled out woman and her departed Christian spouse, *the loss is not forever!* Where he has gone, I will also go.

Why didn't Jesus give us more details about what it is like in the presence of God? Possibly because eternity and our immortal life will be so different from our earthly concepts that no vocabulary could adequately describe it.

Because He didn't spell it out, we don't know what kind of relationships we will have in heaven with those whom we have known here on earth. It seems clear that we will recognize each other and retain our identities. Jesus stated that in the resurrection "there will be no marrying or giving in marriage," (Mark 12:25) but we don't know what that really means. Whatever it will be like, we can be sure God has planned it perfectly for His glory and our satisfaction.

But he wasn't finished!

Whatever the circumstances surrounding your husband's death—illness or accident—however precious or difficult your relationship, whatever happiness or unhappiness he experienced on earth, *it is as nothing* compared to the joy and freedom *he is experiencing now.* As a redeemed and immortal child of God, he is now in the presence of Jesus Christ.

Whenever anyone's time comes to step over *The Finish Line*, he leaves personal plans, tasks, ambitions, dreams and ministry goals *incomplete* according to *our* limited, human opinion. We may be sad to think about all that our husbands still wanted to enjoy and accomplish. We may protest, "But he had so much to live for!"

We struggle with the words "finished, completed, fulfilled." They seem to imply that everything gets all wrapped up in a satisfactory final package—accomplished, achieved, realized, successfully attained. It doesn't.

Who of us would ever feel that we were done or finished in the sense of not having anything left to do or to dream? We are consumed with our own plans, our doings.

If our lives were over today, we might feel that our mapped-out personal goals would dangle like loose ends under a weaver's shuttle. We view our lives from the underside; God looks at them from above, from the perspective of eternity. He sees the finished design according to *His original plan.* Length of life doesn't seem relevant then, does it? God is not bound by time.

I don't fully understand what that means, but it makes me wonder if I might be nearly finished with God's assignment and not realize it. My personal, unachieved goals may not be important when compared to God's plan.

In the case of our Christian husbands, we may think their lives and plans were "cut short" by death, whether they died at an early age or advanced age. But this cannot be true from God's side. We need to believe that their course on earth really *was finished.* Not aborted. Not terminated earlier than God planned it. God wouldn't allow anything to happen until *He is finished* with His work through His son or daughter.

Our death is just as meticulously planned as the death of Christ. Evil men, disease, or accident cannot come to us as long as God has work for us to do. We die according to God's timetable and not ours. . . . No believer who walks with God dies until his work is finished, until his "hour" has come.[4]

Therefore, I accept God's decision that my husband reached His perfect Finish Line first. It was God's responsibility, not my husband's, to accomplish what concerned him. What God began in our husbands' lives He finished—in His perfect time frame. Jesus is the

Alpha and the Omega, the beginning and the end. "[Christ] ... shall also confirm you to the end..." (1 Corinthians 1:8).

"For we are His workmanship, created in Christ Jesus for good works, which God prepared beforehand, that we should walk in them" (Eph. 2:10). God's plans involving your husband and mine were "prepared beforehand" with their names on them. Fantastic! And He has a set of plans like that for you and me, too! God doesn't expect us to be *successful*, as the world looks at success. He calls us to be *faithful* to what *He* planned for us to do.

> The Lord will accomplish what concerns me; Thy lovingkindness, O Lord, is everlasting; Do not forsake the works of Thy hands (Psalm 138:8).
>
> I will cry to God Most High, to God who accomplishes all things for me (Psalm 57:2).
>
> For I am confident of this very thing, that He who began a good work in you will perfect it until the day of Christ Jesus (Philippians 1:6).

So—not to worry. Not to regret. Our husbands did *not* die "prematurely" no matter what their age, or what they might have been in the process of doing or wanting to do. If we are Christians, God has His hands on the steering wheel of our lives. He lovingly holds the stopwatch. If Satan is trying to persuade us by false whispers that our husbands' lives were "aborted," we shouldn't listen.

We must anchor ourselves in God's Word. It will keep our fragile boat from capsizing with doubts and regrets. Let's hold hands with each other and trust God for the things we don't know or understand.

Letting go is a process

But how about my relationship to my husband *now?* Am I still a married woman with loyalty and ties to my husband who has died? Many of us understandably feel that we want to and should continue to be loyal to our spouses even after they have died. That uneasiness can keep us from moving on to what God still wants to do in and through us. It pulls us backward. We may eventually be ready to gently close the door to the past, but we are reluctant to *lock* it.

Isn't loyalty commendable? Natural? The truth is, *I am no longer married.* Scripturally, I'm under no obligation, even loving obligation, to my former husband. As much as I might like to continue our commitment to each other, that commitment is no longer valid. "A wife is bound *as long as her husband lives;* but if her husband is dead, she is free...." (1 Corinthians 7:39). My husband no longer has authority over me, (1 Corinthians 7:4) nor, in his immortal state, would he want to have any. Our relationship is dissolved. It doesn't exist anymore. Legal bonds are severed as well.

It's hard for us to emotionally internalize the biblical truth that *we are not married any longer.* But our mutual marriage pledge, "Till death do us part" was completed. *Death did part us.*

Lifelong loyalty, yes, while both of us were living. *Leftover loyalty* to a spouse now in heaven, no. Emotional bonds are invisible but strong, so it is not easy to let go. That truth is more difficult to grasp emotionally than mentally. The fact is, I should let my husband go, say a loving goodbye. This may sound so abrupt and even harsh to a grieving spouse in the early throes of loss and adjustment. But *a new relationship with the Lord* lies joyfully ahead beyond the tears.

Transfer of ownership

I may feel in limbo after my husband died, feeling that I no longer *belong* to anyone. I belonged to my husband before. Do I belong only to myself now?

The Bible states, "You are not your own" (1 Corinthians 6:19-20). "You belong to Christ" (1 Corinthians 3:23). *So—I belong to Christ!* The Holy Spirit lives in my body, and I am a temple. Jesus bought me with an incredibly high price by giving His own life for me.

I see my singled out life in an entirely new light. Ownership of my body has now been transferred to the Lord! As a Christian, of course I belonged to Him already, but as far as earthly relationship, obligations and responsibilities, I belonged to my husband. Now I'm released from my husband's bonds to form *an even stronger bond with the Lord* to whom I now belong *exclusively.* He pledges Himself to me, and I pledge myself to Him not for the years of time alone, but *for Eternity!* When my new loyalty is transferred to the Lord, a new life and a new assignment lie ahead!

My feeling of incompleteness

As I emerge into "real life" again, I encounter an unexpected dilemma. When I'm in a group that my husband and I were a part of as a couple, I find myself feeling incomplete, unsure of my own identity. Before, I seemed to draw my identity from his.

I am still who I am and who I was. My husband's absence doesn't change my identity. The very phrase "separated by death" says it all. I don't feel whole. I feel like the leftover half of what had been a oneness, when two had become one. Now I am a single *one* again.

If I dwell on that point, I falsely convince myself that I'm no longer a whole person, that I lack something basic. But as a Christian, a Scriptural truth overrules that feeling. *I am complete in Christ.* (Colossians 2:10) If I was a Christian before I married, I did not give up that completeness when I married. Spiritually, both my husband and I were complete. Two complete-in-Christ persons became one. When one leaves by death, it doesn't leave the other a *half-person or incomplete.*

A friend who was beginning to recognize her completeness in spite of her widowhood put it this way: "Now new acquaintances are finally beginning to relate to me *as me,* not as half of a demolished pair."

Some wives allow themselves to become so dependent upon their husbands that rather than confessing with Paul, "For me to live is Christ" (Philippians 1:21) they should more accurately admit, "For me to live is my husband." When her husband dies, such a woman's life doesn't seem worth living to her. Biblically, her previous attitude while married was off balance.

Of course a special closeness exists between husbands and wives. They naturally depend on one another.

That is good and right, and their lives should be inter-twined. But neither spouse should give up his or her completeness in Christ.

Easier said than done. But first biblically, then intellectually, finally emotionally I should realize that I am truly "complete in Christ." Not half-a-person. "In Him [Christ] we live and move and exist" (Acts 17:28).

New Principles

In the New Testament we are given specific coun-sel about our new state as singled out women. Key passages are found in the seventh chapter of First Corinthians, verses 8, 29-31, 39,40 (NIV). In them the apostle Paul gives general principles for the married, the no-longer-married and those who never married.

A woman is bound to her husband as long as he lives. But if her husband dies, she is free to marry anyone she wishes, but he must belong to the Lord. In my judgment, she is happier if she stays as she is—and I think that I too have the Spirit of God. . . . Now to the unmarried and the widows I say: It is good for them to stay unmarried, as I am. . . time is short. From now on those who have wives should live as if they had none; those who mourn, as if they did not; those who are happy, as if they were not; those who buy something, as if it were not theirs to keep; those who use the things of the world, as if not engrossed in them. For this world in its present form is passing away.

This passage gives us a sound biblical premise for our new state. What are the practical implications and personal principles for me?

❦ My marriage bonds are only for this earthly life.
❦ As a widow, I am not married anymore.
❦ I may marry again.
❦ The condition for remarriage is that my new husband should be a Christian.
❦ I may be happier not to remarry.
❦ I now regain authority over my own body under God.
❦ Whether married or unmarried, I should live with the view that time is short, and the world system is temporary.
❦ If I mourn, I should not let grief overwhelm me, and I should move on.
❦ I should keep happiness, too, in perspective.
❦ I should not be preoccupied with the acquisition of possessions and their use.

God will show each of us how to flesh out her new freedoms in her walk with Christ and how to carry out her fresh assignment more fruitfully and joyfully. On what should I then focus my concern? Paul wanted widowed believers to be *free from encumbrances* in serving the Lord.

I would like you to be free from concern. . . . An unmarried woman or virgin is concerned about the Lord's affairs: Her aim is to be devoted to the Lord in both body and spirit. But a married woman is concerned about the affairs of this world—how she can please her husband. I am saying this for your own good, not to restrict you, but that you may live in a right way in undivided devotion to the Lord (1 Corinthians 7:32-35 NIV).

Some conclusions for us singled out women from the above passage:

❦ I should concern myself primarily about the Lord's affairs.

❦ My goal should be devotion to the Lord (*be holy,* in other translations) in both body and spirit.

❦ Concern for the affairs of this world and pleasing my husband are no longer on my agenda.

❦ I receive new freedom so that I may express undivided devotion to the Lord.

My new focus and center should clearly be toward the Lord, how to please Him in all I say and do. Second Corinthians 5:9 defines my new motivation, "So we make it our goal to please Him. . . . "

Is that the honest desire of my heart? If I'm not sure how I should please the Lord, I should follow Paul's counsel in Ephesians 5:10, ". . . *find out* what pleases the Lord." The better I know anyone, including the Lord, the more I know what pleases him. Colossians 1:10-12 NIV provides me with at least a beginner's list of what pleases the Lord.

And we pray this in order that you may live a life worthy of the Lord *and may please him in every way*: bearing fruit in every good work, growing in the knowledge of God, being strengthened with all power according to his glorious might so that you may have great endurance and patience, and joyfully giving thanks to the Father, who has qualified you to share in the inheritance of the saints in the kingdom of light.

What a grand description of what God expects of us as singled out women! We're now free to devote all our time, efforts and love toward becoming conformed to the image of the Lord who has captured our hearts and loves us with an everlasting love. That certainly doesn't mean that we should live a cloistered life of withdrawal from the world. The characteristics Paul listed develop in the thick of everyday life with its problems, activities and opportunities.

To be practical, if we're no longer married, should we continue to wear a wedding ring? That's a personal matter, only a cultural custom, not a spiritual matter. It is not even a tradition for most of the world's people.

Even in our society the custom of wearing wedding bands isn't uniformly followed. Since the Bible says I'm not married any longer, wearing a wedding band or not doesn't seem significant. I'm not disloyal to my husband if I don't continue to wear a wedding band because my husband is no longer married to me. He is beyond marriage as we know it.

If I wish to continue wearing my wedding ring, it will no longer be a symbol that I'm married. It will only be a memento of a past relationship. Each of us is free to decide.

Home at last

Ted and I traveled the world in ministry. Our ocean crossings by plane were multiple. When we were away from home for an extended time, we'd get tired of sleeping in different beds each night in strange parts of the world. We would jokingly remind each other while traveling in some far off village in the countryside of China, "No one in the world knows where we are at this moment. We could drop out of sight, and no one would know what happened to us. Only God knows where we are!"

The time would always come when we'd say, "Enough. Let's go home!" Sometimes we'd even cut short our trip. We were homesick. We quickly packed and turned our hearts and steps (or flight) toward home.

The closer our plane came to the United States, the more eager we became. During the final hour-and-a-half drive from Dulles International Airport we were always restless with anticipation. When we turned into our subdivision, then into our driveway and hurried up the steps and through the front door, we would sigh with joy and relief that *we were finally home.*

When we returned from our last trip to Europe, we sent a cable to my relatives in the Czech Republic with only two words: *"Jsme doma."* (We're home) Short and sweet and economical! They would understand and be relieved that we arrived safely.

Now Ted is *home.* He is not in a strange place, even though he had never been there before. Jesus, whom he loved and served for a lifetime and talked with every day, warmly welcomed him. I don't think my husband had to fix up the place, though he loved to do that on earth. If Jesus said He was "going to prepare a place for you," it can't be less than perfect and comfortable. It is I who have to fix up the home into which I moved after Ted's death.

My husband is surely in the company of many others whom he knew on earth, who probably had a joyful "Welcome Home!" party for him. He belongs there. I'm sure he made himself at home from day one.

Since I am anchored in this biblical truth, what reason do I have to mourn or grieve *for him?* Do I get tired of reminding myself that the grief I feel is *for myself?* No, I need the reminder. *I'm* not "home" yet. 🕊️

Relationships are even more important to me as a singled out woman. Now they are the glowing part of my life where I warm my cold hands and heart. I need "people with skin on" to talk with, to hug, be hugged by and grow with!

6   *Refocusing My Relationships*

 *R*elationships assume different roles than when I was part of a married couple, half a parent couple and grandparent duo. *I am now a single parent, no matter how old I am!* Both sides of family relationships need to learn how to adjust.

My children are not my husband

Without our husbands to look to for security and emotional needs, we may look to our children, especially the adult ones, for emotional fulfillment. We are tempted to lean more heavily on them, to intrude in their lives more than we did when our husbands were living.

We take for granted that they, more than anyone else, should understand us and fill the gaps in our incomplete lives. We may feel emotionally disintegrated and instinctively look to them for our wholeness. We may even expect them to take over our decision making, to become spouse-figures for us.

Some adult children become solicitous and thrive on such an enhanced role. Some become oversolicitous and smother their newly-widowed mother, stifling her initiative. Some make all her decisions and thus atrophy her strength. This does not apply to the early days and weeks after our loss when we do need many strong shoulders to lean on.

Sometimes adult children withdraw emotionally, even keeping their distance, because they honestly don't know how to relate to and support their mother. Having lost a father, they struggle with their own grief. They, too, need comfort and adjustment before they can help their mother cope.

Unless we are permanently incapacitated, either physically or mentally, we should stand on our own feet and lean on God for support and decision making. Although we still need warm bodies to relate to, we must not let our children assume an improper role in our lives or force them into it.

I must remember that I, the spouse, am not the only one affected by the loss of my husband. My adult children, grand-children, his siblings, extended family, friends, co-workers and others were part of his life.

I'm inclined to think only of myself, my loss, adjustment, future and emotions. Each of the others has his own orbit of loss and needs to work through grief toward acceptance and adjustment at his own pace.

Stay an outsider

Staying an outsider in our adult or married children's lives seems wise. Unless extreme conditions dictate, living in their homes is not advisable, especially if grandchildren are involved. We must be realistic, however. Sometimes living with or near our family is necessary or appropriate.

Two or three generations under one roof isn't usually a recipe for harmony under the best conditions. Schedules, discipline, habits, lifestyles and activities differ generationally. The times my sons live in now are not like when they lived under our roof.

Most adult children are relieved and happy when mom has a life and friends and interests of her own. A good rule is, "Where you are much wanted, go little; where you are little wanted, go not at all." Let *your family* extend the invitation.

Moving in with one's children usually compounds a widow's problems. Managing the kitchen together is awkward. A mother's or mother-in-law's "takeover" is seldom a good thing even if your intention is to lift the wife's load. Remember, it is not *your* home. Their lives are theirs to live. A few rules of thumb may help us when we visit our adult children and their families:

- Wait for an invitation.
- Don't tell them what to do or how to do it.
- Be available when needed.
- Keep thy mouth shut.
- Help cheerfully when asked.
- Be quick to affirm the positive.
- Don't point out what you would do differently.
- Stay out of the way of their routine and schedules.
- Don't preach. Simply live a Jesus-life.
- Don't manipulate or take sides.
- Treat your grown children like adult friends, not your little kids.

❦ Let them have their privacy.
❦ Don't show favoritism among the grandchildren.
❦ Love freely with no strings attached.
❦ Don't overstay your welcome.

Physical contact

A few months after my husband died, our son, Gary, and his wife, Theresa, gently insisted that I leave the scene of my loss and spend a month with their family in another state. I was reluctant, preferring to stay home and get on with my on-site adjustment. Finally they prevailed.

One of the first genuine therapy treatments they initiated (I'm sure they didn't think of it as therapy) was not to let me say goodnight and go to my room without their hugs. They sprinkled other spontaneous hugs generously throughout my stay.

I didn't realize how much I needed that physical contact. I lapped it up and looked forward to it, greatly missing that sweet expression of love when I returned to live alone. However, my other sons and families continue to fill the hug gap whenever we are together.

I've become more of a giver and receiver of hugs since my loss. How much we all need physical contact! The apostle Paul repeated his admonition, "Brethren, greet one another with a holy kiss," in five of his letters to the young churches. A kiss was a customary greeting in those days, similar to our modern handshake. Justin Martyr (A.D. 150) recorded that the holy kiss was a regular part of early worship services. They still practice it in the churches of some other cultures.

Sometimes in a phone conversation, especially with another singled out friend, I suggest that my call is a long distance hug. How it warms both of our hearts even over the phone lines!

I copied the following from a health magazine while sitting in a doctor's office:

> ❦ Hugging is healthy: It helps the immune system, cures depression, reduces stress, induces sleep.
> ❦ It's invigorating, rejuvenating and has no unpleasant side effects.
> ❦ Hugging is nothing less than a miracle drug.
> ❦ Hugging is all natural: It is organic, naturally sweet, no pesticides, no preservatives, no artificial ingredients and 100 percent wholesome.
> ❦ Hugging is practically perfect: There are no movable parts, no batteries to wear out, no periodic checkups, low energy consumption, high energy yield, inflation-proof, nonfattening, no monthly payments, no insurance requirements, theft-proof, non-taxable and non-polluting.
> ❦ Of course, hugging is *fully returnable.* [1]

Sherry, a Christian nurse friend, told me she makes it a practice in her hospital rounds to deliberately touch a patient's hand, shoulder or foot (discretely, of course) as she checks on their condition. She found it to be a healthy gesture appreciated by most patients. Human beings seem to thrive on the warmth of touch at any age.

Solitary confinement

Although masked by my busy work, loneliness is ever-present. Sometimes I'm lonely even with people around. I'm especially lonely when they leave. Nights are lonely. Evenings hang heavy with aloneness. My husband and I spent most evenings together although we pursued separate activities. Weekends are lonely and charged with memories of things we did together.

I saw myself slipping toward isolation in the early days and weeks while emerging from the shock period. Home was secure and familiar. I didn't need to explain myself or put on any facade of courage.

It's so easy to drift into the habit of staying at home. I catch myself making excuses and declining invitations to accompany friends to activities, church and leisure pursuits. If I'm not careful, I can sentence myself to prison, even to solitary confinement. Others do not lock me in. I walk into that cell by my own choice and close the door. I can vegetate unnecessarily. *I have the key in my pocket* with freedom to "go in and out and find pasture" as Jesus said in John 10:9.

What is this key in my pocket? Balance in my life with sufficient time alone and then blocks of time with people so that I can take advantage of God's entire pasture land.

What does it mean to *find pasture?* It implies food, nourishment and rest. The beautiful song, *"People need the Lord"* expresses it so honestly. I'm one of those people. How I need the Lord as my Shepherd! His presence is vital to me, especially as I work through my new singled out status. I must spend time with Him so I can grow strong again and discern what He wants of me.

I'm not embarrassed to admit that I need
friends and the flow of people around
me. Sheep are not loners, but part of a
flock. I need to rub wool with God's other
sheep in His pasture.

I need to pick out an event or activity that interests
me and then find a friend with whom to go. Others may be
just as shy or unwilling to take a risk. We can meet half
way.

It takes effort and initiative, however. If no one
calls me, instead of sitting around feeling neglected,
forgotten and lonely, I should pick up the phone and call
someone. I shouldn't be afraid of rejection or presuming on
people. Gradually I'm starting to invite people to my home.
I'm trying new activities—even becoming adventurous!

Loneliness is not a deep pit in which I'm permanently stuck. I have a ladder against the side up which I
may climb to rejoin the world. However, I must do the
climbing.

Filling the friendship gap

Where are those friends with whom I can talk and
share feelings, to whom I can give and from whom I may
receive love? We need to recognize that no other human
being can completely fill our need. A friend sent me a
quotation from Elisabeth Elliot: "Too often we ask of
people what they cannot give—security, strength, satisfaction. God did not design people to give these things to

each other. We need to seek them from Jesus."

Some of us find a measure of human support within our church family. Some do not. Support groups are available for those who have lost spouses. Participation in them works for some but not for others. Each of us needs to find her own way at different stages of her new journey.

I don't want people to pity me. I don't
need people to "befriend" me. I need
people to *be* friends with me.

I have different circles of friends. Some are casual acquaintances—we speak but don't connect. With others I have stimulating, worthwhile conversations. However, only a few are confidants with whom I can bare my soul without fear of embarrassment or judgment. I seek friends with positive attitudes.

Blessed are we if we have at least one "good buddy" who is by our side when we need her, if not in person, then by phone or letter.

A common dread for some newly singled out women is to go places and do things alone, especially places where we formerly went as a couple. Some of my friends refuse to go to a restaurant alone.

By temperament, I am self-conscious and shy, so I had to work on being outgoing. Eventually I discovered a way to offset my discomfort. If I go to a fast-food restaurant, I look for another person (of my own sex and usually in my age bracket) who is also alone. I send up a quick prayer for the Lord's guidance in this uncertain adventure. I try to sit near her and force myself (because this does not come naturally) to take the initiative. I open with some trivial, friendly comment (even weather!) and encourage conversation. If I encounter a blank wall, no response, that's all right. I've tried. I sit alone.

More often than not, the lady sitting alone invites me to her table. I express genuine interest in her. I forget about myself in the discovery of another person's interests or problems. I also do this in my frequent travels, realizing I'll probably never see that person again. Usually we don't even exchange names, although we talk like old friends. It's amazing what personal things we can discuss in a situation like that. And how freely I can share with a perfect stranger, what Christ means to me when God gives such an opening in our conversation.

Several such encounters resulted in exchanging names and addresses, and we corresponded for a while encouraging each another.

Why should I avoid the company of couples? The fifth-wheel syndrome is only in my head. If I don't make something of it, it doesn't matter.

Surely God doesn't exclusively favor even numbers—2, 4, 6 and 8. He also created 1, 3, 5 and 7. A fifth wheel is very important if you have a flat tire!

Couples continue to be great company for us who are singled out. I shouldn't make them feel uncomfortable that they are having a good time and, poor me, I'm not, because I don't have a mate. It's up to me whether I'm good company or not. Yes, sorrow colors life. Nevertheless, what color, is up to me.

To eat alone need not be a big deal. The Lord is always the unseen host at my table, my Most Significant Other, whether I'm home alone or having a hamburger somewhere in public. Why should I be embarrassed that my husband left me for heaven? It wasn't for another woman!

I feel vulnerable, however. I test potential relationships so I won't be emotionally hurt or disappointed. I open my heart-door only a crack at first to see whether a person is sensitive to my emotional state or is simply a busy-time person who will offer shallow sympathy, ignore my needs or not even attempt to understand.

As I put out feelers toward those I allow into my life, I seek those who will respond and help me grow in Christ along with them. I must take the initiative to invite such people into my life. My son, Gary, wisely encouraged, "Mom, open yourself to closeness."

I don't need to restrict my friendships to my age group. I'm excited when God brings into my life new and refreshing relationships at either end of the age spectrum and from both sexes. We older singles can delightfully expand our horizons by friendship with those who are younger.

Most books about adjusting to the loss of a spouse point out that there is nothing wrong with having men as friends without any romantic involvement. It's important to have some mutual understanding so that you are both on the same wave length in such friendships. When you join groups or activities, there may be opportunities to meet men who fall into the category of pals rather than potential marriage partners. It's emotionally healthy to have men friends in our lives whether or not we are open to marriage. Because fewer demands are put on both parties, such relationships tend to be more open, balanced and mutually beneficial.

Enlarging my circle of friends to include the companionship of both men and women helps me build a foundation for getting back into the mainstream of social contacts.

I don't want to nurture friendships with people whom the Lord doesn't want in my new life. Not always having the wisdom to discern that, I ask the Lord to give me insight. I try to surround myself with people I like, whose friendships are meaningful, and who minister to me or to whom I may minister. Friendship is not a one-way street.

Remarriage possibilities

A word of caution, however. As newly singled out women, we are particularly vulnerable emotionally. Tragic situations can develop when a widow too quickly jumps into another marriage, especially before she has made her way fully through the healthy grieving process

and adjusted to her new status. Our eagerness for closeness may blind us. Our desire to escape from our loneliness may push us into remarriage prematurely. Remember that both parties have a lifetime of established habits
and experiences behind them, and a new union including
two extended families is not easy under the best of
conditions. Both parties carry more baggage of all sorts
into a second marriage. Keep your eyes wide open and
your heart under control. Watch out for caution signals.

The apostle Paul instructed that a widow should
marry "only in the Lord." Even when both parties are
Christians, there is no guarantee of a melding of temperaments, interests and life goals. One author advised:

> After your spouse has been deceased for
> a period of time, you may think about the
> possibility of once again sharing your life with
> another. We do not wish to imply that all
> survivors should start an immediate search for
> a new mate. Many well-adjusted people may
> never desire to marry again. All knowledge-
> able people are well aware that marriage does
> not necessarily equal happiness, and it is bet-
> ter to be alone than to be involved in an unsat-
> isfactory marriage. Trust in God to direct your
> path.
>
> Having common interests such as hob-
> bies and leisure-time activities and similar
> value systems, including political views and
> moral and spiritual values, is important. Much
> of the success of marriage is based on spending
> time together in conversation and on activities
> that both parties appreciate. Considerable com-

mon ground should be found, and the parties should communicate openly on the major issues of life. [2]

Settle it in your own mind that you will never find a new mate exactly like your first husband. Your new husband will no doubt have some good and some less-than-good qualities that your first mate did not have. Don't place your former mate on a pedestal and challenge your new partner to climb up on the same pedestal. Nor is there profit in amplifying all the faults of your former spouse. Be fair and objective. What happened in your first marriage is history—let it go at that.

In many cases remarriages work out well. The couple needs to realize that their relationship will *take work*. When God is central in each of their lives, when they have individually worked through their past and made healthy adjustments, and they have many compatibilities, such a marriage has a good chance to succeed.

My need to be needed

During my married and childbearing and child-raising years, I was needed, depended on, leaned on by others. I was necessary to them. When the child-dependency stage ended and the empty nest stage began, my husband still needed me. I was not out of my accustomed orbit.

After my husband died, I felt as if no one depended on me or needed me. I floated in limbo like an astronaut whose tether has been severed from the mother ship.

Throughout my life, my self-worth seemed bound up in *doing* for others. My productive urge is still strong, even in my widowhood. Friends and family keep advising, "Be good to yourself for a change." I find that attitude difficult. I'll have to work on it, nevertheless I still need the serving-others role. I need people to need me, and I want to be useful in some way to God. I should not tie my self-worth to productiveness, however, nor consider my worth to God as dependent on my works.

The Lord is more interested in my *being*—who I am—than my *doing*. I need to keep reminding myself of that basic truth.

Fellow travelers

I'm drawn like the needle on a compass to those who have gone down this single road before. Until my own loss, I'm sorry to say I tried to avoid people who lost loved ones because I didn't know what to say. Now I eagerly search for such people. What the Lord has taught them becomes valuable to me. They can point out pitfalls ahead, and they can direct me to the joys. They've walked the path that is so untried and new to me.

Many of them reach out to me, and I sense their guileless compassion. Now I must express my compassion by reaching to others who are joining us on this once-again-single journey. I'm eager to hold hands and share my heart with them, to hug them and walk with them. I want to listen to them, share their experience, pray with and for them.

Now I understand compassion in shoe leather. "Each of you should look not only to your own interests, but also to the interests of others" (Philippians 2:4 NIV). I must look to the needs of my sisters who are traveling the same path.

If the Lord is helping me to adjust in a certain area, and my sister is having struggles, perhaps failing, whether she is a beginner or a discouraged trudger on the long road, I am to build her up. (Romans 15:1,2) She, in turn, encourages me when I am weak and uncertain.

We must walk softly when giving advice to one another as we go through the grieving process. It was no comfort to me when someone said, "There are tragedies greater than yours." Or, "At least you are alive." Connie, a singled out friend who is sensitive and emotional by temperament, told me how hurt she was when someone told her, "It's time you stopped feeling bad." One author gave good advice:

> Mourners taught me a lesson. They don't want answers from their friends. They want companionship while they seek their own answers: searching their hearts, exploring their religious values, reexamining their philosophy of life, reviving their coping resources and rearranging their whole view of the future.
>
> During this radical process, the best of their friends will simply stand with them and whisper "Amen" as grievers utter their own version of the Serenity Prayer: "Lord, help me to accept the things I cannot change, to change the things I can, and the wisdom to know the difference." [3]

My personal pushups

It's painful when someone reminds me that my husband is no longer here to take care of me, and that I shouldn't lean on my children. Nevertheless, it is realistic.

Some relationships proved disappointing to me after Ted's death. I took for granted that certain people would rally to my need. They failed to do so. The solicitous attention that surrounded me during the immediacy of my loss drastically thinned out in time. The sympathy cards arrived less frequently and finally stopped coming. The phone seldom rang. Life went on as usual for everyone else, and I, too, had to move on. Ultimately I was responsible for myself.

The hymn writer put it sensitively: "When other helpers fail and comforts flee, Help of the helpless, Lord, abide with me." My Lord has not left me. He is in me, and I am in Him. What David did, I must learn to do: "David *encouraged himself* in the Lord" (1 Samuel 30:6).

I must learn to nourish myself spiritually, to eat God's Word for myself, encourage myself with His promises and appropriate His love for me.

I need to practice my own spiritual, mental and emotional push ups and pull ups. As I draw my strength directly from God, I grow stronger and more healthy spiritually.

The most important part of my daily spiritual nutrition regime is to draw near to God, seek His face and allow His Holy Spirit to be my Comforter and Encourager.

Church relationships

"I would *never* have thought of changing churches!" declared Myra, who has been a widow for many years. She and her husband were members of one church for most of their married lives. They sat in the same pew every Sunday, had the same circle of church friends, and for decades were involved in that church's activities.

Lois, another singled out friend, enthusiastically stated that changing churches was one of the *first* things she felt God wanted her to do after her husband died. She was happy and invigorated to make new friends and become involved in fresh service and activities. In her new church they accepted her for herself, a new member in her own right, rather than the widow of someone they had known so well. She was eager to set off not only on a life of her own but on a church life of her own as part of a new church family.

Each of us should make that decision after much prayer and with a clear head. Most of us don't think very clearly immediately after our husband's death. We should not make such an important personal decision hastily. Some churches take seriously the covenant community principle, and we should be careful and prayerful about changing our church affiliation in such cases. If we have a continuing obligation to teach or serve, we should consider that carefully.

Polly is a widow who felt led to remain in her church, but she decided not to sit in the same pew that she had shared with her husband. She chose different opportunities for service within her church instead of continuing those in which she and her husband had been active as a couple.

The choice may depend on the degree of ease with which we make new friends. If we choose a new church, we must take the initiative to be friendly because we are the outsiders. A different fellowship of Christians may be like a fresh breeze to our spirits at a time when we are looking to the Lord for our new assignment. We need to be sensitive to obey His new directions. Whether we make a change, will also depend on whether we relocate and at what distance.

A change of churches is not for everyone. Some do best and continue to grow spiritually in the security of a familiar place of worship, in the warmth of cultivated close friendships and in an already established loving community of believers.

If we decide to join a new church, let's not make a big to-do about being widows. Really, *it doesn't show*—except that we usually arrive alone.

We want people to accept us because of who we are in Christ, not that we have lost our spouse. Every group of believers not only has its own statement of faith, but its own characteristics of worship and fellowship. Let us pray to find the specific place where the Lord wants to replant us, or be sure where He wants us to stay.

We need to be in a church where we can grow in Christ by being nurtured from the Word and through fellowship with other believers—and a place where we can become involved in service as the Lord leads. The right church family gives us a sense of belonging, one of our important needs as singled out women.

Let's bloom wherever the Lord plants us!

When tears surprise us, let's not look at them as puddles in the potholes on Adjustment Avenue, but as creating bridges made of rainbows. Our tears are the rain, and God's love is the sunshine filtering through the storm clouds. The result is a rainbow bridge! Let's embrace the tears, and then move on over the rainbow bridge to what lies ahead.

Potholes on
7 *Adjustment Avenue*

*A*djustment Avenue for the singled out woman is not a smooth, yellow brick road. It's full of potholes.

Nothing is easy as we reenter the "real" world after the seeming unreality of the death of our spouses. Certain adjustments, particularly emotional ones, are more difficult than others, and require a struggle before victory. I've isolated some of the more common emotions. They are from my experience, but I believe you can readily identify with them.

I feel two opposing forces within. On one hand, I'm inclined to let my emotions loose; on the other, I try to suppress and mask my emotions, hiding under a cloak of courage and strength.

Both negative and positive possibilities lie in our emotions. As grieving spouses, we usually focus on negatives—anger, guilt, depression, fear, loneliness, denial, anguish—grief itself. However, some emotions are positive: peace, joy, love, patience, compassion and others which come as the fruit of the Holy Spirit. We can grow those fruits even while we walk through the valley of the shadow of death.

Peace? I accept it from God to cancel my anguish. Joy? For Ted's new state and a caring God who has plans

for me. Love? Coupled with compassion for other suffer-
ers going through similar experiences.

Flash floods

Words scrolling across the bottom of the screen
interrupted a TV program—our area was under a flash
flood watch. Streams were swollen and high water made
some highways impassable. Storm drains couldn't carry
off the torrential rain and melting snow. The ground
reached saturation level.

My emotions, too, are at flash flood level after the
death of my husband. When they reach the saturation
point, my tears flow.

- Tears come at predictable times or take
  me by surprise.
- They overtake me when I'm alone or in
  public.
- Frustration, panic or confusion can set
  them off.
- Sometimes no apparent reason triggers
  them.
- Working through my questions and
  searching for answers brings tears.
- When surrendering my struggles into
  God's hands, I may cry.

Crying has two aspects: emotional expression with
visible tears, on one hand, and crying-prayer, on the
other. Most "crying" recorded in the Bible is the latter.
God listens to tears, visible or unseen, just as He listens
to and understands perfectly the "groaning which cannot
be uttered" of the Holy Spirit when He intercedes for us.

God hears our groaning when we "know not what to pray for as we ought." (Romans 8:26,27) "Crying unto the Lord" is spiritually therapeutic.

As recorded in 2 Kings 20:1-3, God notified King Hezekiah that his illness was terminal. He turned his face to the wall, wept and prayed. I can sympathize with that. Jeremiah, the prophet, couldn't deliver a message from God without erupting in tears. Countless strong men of God whose stories we read in the Scriptures shed tears. Chuck Swindoll commented:

> When words fail, tears flow. Tears have a language all their own, a tongue that needs no interpreter. In some mysterious way, our complex inner-communication system knows when to admit its verbal limitations ... and the tears come.
>
> Eyes that flashed and sparkled only moments before are flooded from a secret reservoir. We try in vain to restrain the flow, but even strong men falter. Tears are not self-conscious. They can spring upon us when we are speaking in public, or standing beside others who look to us for strength. Most often they appear when our soul is overwhelmed with feelings that words cannot describe.[1]

When tears surprise us, let's not look at them as puddles in the potholes on Adjustment Avenue, but as *creating bridges made of rainbows.* Our tears are the rain, and God's love is the sunshine filtering through the storm clouds. The result is a rainbow bridge! Let's embrace the tears, and then move on over the rainbow bridge to what lies ahead.

Never let them see you sweat (cry)?

A TV commercial for deodorant warns, "Never let them see you sweat!" When I apply that to holding in my emotions as a pretense of bravado, that's bad advice. Suppression acts like a pressure cooker with a plugged steam valve. Eventually I'll explode. Like a balloon into which I continue to blow air beyond its capacity, eventually I'll burst. Like a can of soda shaken and shaken, when I flip the tab, I'll spurt out my pent-up emotions.

I learned the lesson the hard way not to suppress my emotions or deny them. Neither should I let them run wild and uncontrolled. I need to welcome positive emotions that rise from my faith, from the sure promises of God in His Word and my lifelong walk with God.

Stress is response to external conditions or *stressors* which upset my equilibrium. The physiological changes that result are called *fight or flight responses,* the body's attempts to deal with perceived danger. Those of us who have lost our spouses, with all the trauma, adjustments and decisions, are prime candidates for some stress-related symptoms.

Stress affects almost every bodily organ and function including the brain, nerves, heart, blood flow, the release of hormones, digestion and muscle function. Some symptoms or side-effects of stress are depression, anxiety, headaches, migraines, insomnia, stomach upset and skin rash. Others are nervousness, rapid heartbeat, elevated blood pressure, diarrhea, constipation and the production of excess stomach acid, which can lead to an ulcer. Not a happy list!

Prolonged stress by bottling up normal grief can lead to more serious illnesses and even emotional or mental imbalance.

I wish someone had told me sooner about all of this. No one did until months later. I became stressed because I worried about becoming ill. I began to notice all kinds of symptoms—heaviness in my chest, breathlessness, an ache that was almost pain. All the symptoms proved groundless, but my imagination ran wild.

Finally, a singled out friend, who was a nurse, tenderly shared her experience with me, alerting me to the health dangers of keeping my grief inside without release. When people asked me how I was doing, I had been answering an automatic "Fine!" Then I tried to force myself to live up to that response and I became stressed. In trying to be courageous and controlled, to show that I "had it together," I didn't give myself enough time to reduce my stress gradually.

The health community advises us to roll with the punches of possible stress by making sure we have outlets such as regular exercise, recreational activities and hobbies. It helps to cultivate friends with whom we can share both our good and bad feelings. We can benefit from relaxation techniques. However, the use of tranquilizers, alcohol or sleeping pills is counterproductive.

As singled out women, let's heed the good advice of David, the poet-king, who must have lived neck deep in stress. In his songs and poems he constantly referred to his *distress*. Synonyms are anguish, agony, trouble, woe, pain, misery, tension—and grief, irritation, affliction and upset. David experienced plenty of that during his long, tumultuous public and private life.

From his writing we see that David
vented his stress in a healthy way. He
repeatedly declared, "In my distress *I
cried unto the Lord.*" He released his
stress directly to One who could do
something about it.

Public wailing and emotional demonstrations, the
custom among pagan people, are not the way to defuse
our stress. In private to my Lord and with close, understanding family or friends, I can be more free with my
true feelings. However, a stiff upper lip and a stoic
attitude are not necessarily Christian.

My friends reminded me repeatedly, "It will take
time." Yes, it *will*. I must dispel my grief gradually, like
letting air slowly out of a tire or balloon. Nevertheless,
"there will be days . . . " they tell me.

Yes, there *are* days when I still need to express my
emotions freely, although considerable time has passed
since my husband's death. It's O.K. I shouldn't feel guilty
about that no matter how much time passes, and neither
should you.

Negative emotions from the Enemy

Some authors of grief books suggest that widows
often feel cheated, especially if their husbands died
young. They may wrestle with that negative emotion.

However, to "cheat" means to take someone else's
property, to deceive, defraud, deprive of something expected. Cheated implies a cheater. How can I say that

about God? By His very nature He is good. I must settle it in my heart that God wouldn't cheat me, and He wouldn't cheat my husband.

After all, my husband wasn't my property. He belonged to the Lord. We expected to grow old together, and I guess, in our case, we did. For that I am thankful. Marriage isn't meant to last forever on earth.

The Devil would like to have us blame God and feel cheated, but we should resist such a suggestion, recognizing where it came from.

Feeling like "the pits"

Another negative emotion the Devil wants to put on us is depression. Most of us have some days when we really do "feel like the pits." We are depressed and discouraged. A friend gave me a large, glossy poster in full color picturing the head of a long-eared, mournful hound with soulful eyes. The caption reads, "I know I'm victorious, Lord, but it sure feels like I'm getting stomped!" That's the way I feel sometimes. My loss and loneliness make me feel stomped on.

A pit is a deep hole like a well. Someone must let you down into it or throw you in. I feel an emotional letdown. The busy activity surrounding my husband's death has diminished. "Pit" is three-fourths of the word "pity" and leads to self-pity. Missionary/author Elisabeth Elliot, twice a widow, tells of her experience:

I try to refuse self-pity. I know of nothing more paralyzing, more deadly. It is a death which has no resurrection, a sinkhole from which no rescuing hand can drag you because you have chosen to sink. But I must refuse it and recognize it for what it is.

Amy Carmichael, in her sword-thrust of a book *If*, writes, "If I make much of anything appointed, magnify it secretly to myself or insidiously to others, then I know nothing of Calvary love." That's a good definition of self-pity—making much of the "appointed," magnifying it, dwelling on one's own losses, looking with envy on those who appear to be more fortunate than oneself, asking "Why me, Lord?" [2]

Today, for instance, is one of those sinkhole days. I feel lethargic from head to toe like a stagnant pond. My mind is sluggish, as if it went on vacation but without the revitalizing benefits. "I am counted with them that go down into the pit: I am as a man that hath no strength" (Psalm 88:4 KJV).

I can think of many reasons for *not* being in the pits. The Lord is so good. Yes, I'm slowly working through my adjustments. I know where my husband is. I know God has kept me alive for some purpose. I'm looking forward to my new assignment. "O Lord, thou hast brought up my soul from the grave; thou hast kept me alive, that I should not go down to the pit" (Psalm 30:3 KJV).

My spiritual life needs recharging. My organ is out of tune. Lord, tune me to Your perfect pitch. I'd like new power and joy and praise to flow through all the pipes of my life.

The way out of my pit is *up*. The rungs of the ladder are obedience and trust in God—as they always are. I must begin by looking upward out of my dark pit into the face of Jesus who has a shining face. "O God, restore us, and cause Thy face to shine upon us, and we will be saved." In Psalm 80 David repeats that verse three times. Lord, bring me out of this emotional depression pit. The sides are slippery. When I'm nearly out, I drop back in. The bottom of the pit is yucky muck. I claim Your promise, "Because he has loved Me, therefore I will deliver him; I will set him securely on high, because he has known My name" (Psalm 90:14).

"He brought me up also out of an horrible pit, out of the miry clay, and set my feet upon a rock, and established my goings" (Psalm 40:2 KJV).

Thanks, Lord, for pushing me up from behind while dropping a heavenly rope down and pulling me out!

Come to my party

As singled out women working through our new adjustments, it's important to get together with our friends. However, we'll find that most people don't want to come to a *pity party.*

Especially when I spend much time alone, I'm inclined to throw such parties. I don't have one every day, but regularly enough to become tiresome, even to me. It usually turns out that I am alone at my party. That's a bummer.

I sit around licking my wounds and pouting. My frown reaches almost to my knees. A *pity party* isn't a fun time for me or anyone else who drops by.

The joy robber, ol' Satan himself, is the only one to arrive on time for my *pity party.* He takes for granted he's invited because he was the one who planted the idea in my mind. He stands at the door with a whole armload of presents wrapped in black, insisting that I let him in.

I'm quite excited until I begin to unwrap them. One is a 3-D gift: depression, discouragement and disappointment. The gift in the biggest box is worry. Another is a box of miscellaneous grumbles and complaints that spill out when I remove the lid. An odd-shaped one is full of imaginations, impatience and "what ifs." They have a bad odor! Satan tied all of them with yellow ribbons of fear.

Satan surprised me by having his best gift delivered by mail—C.O.D. to boot! It was *self-pity,* all wrapped up in itself. I can't believe I had to pay to receive it!

Satan is disappointed because I don't like his gifts. He wants me to keep them anyway for a future *pity party,* in case no one else will bring gifts. He tries to please me with one final gift—a mirror. He urges me to take a good look at myself.

Poor me! What a low self-image I reflect! He cackles with glee to see the pout on my face. How dejected and neglected I feel! I really look like a widow now. Satan urges me to pull down the curtains and give up.

I feel so low I don't even want Satan around. *I demand that he leave my party.*

That's one order he has to obey, according to James 4:7, "Resist the devil and he will flee from you."

As he bolts out the door, that joy robber taunts me by singing the little children's ditty: "Nobody loves me, everybody hates me, guess I'll go eat worms!"

Gloom settles over the room, and a stench lingers. *Another knock on the door.*

Oh, it's God. I forgot to invite Him, but He came anyway. He brought an enormous basket carefully gift wrapped in gold paper. Will I accept it, He asks?

I thank Him and unwrap it to find it filled with beautiful fruit of the Spirit. (Galatians 5:22,23) The pleasant, mellow aroma is almost overwhelming. I take the fruit out and put it on the party table where I stacked Satan's gifts. Magically, Satan's gifts vanish! Sunshine floods the room, and a spring fragrance floats in on a fresh breeze.

God is pleased. "I have one more gift for you." He hands me a mirror. *Oh no, not another mirror!* However, when I look into God's mirror, things look different! I see myself as a child of God created in the image of Jesus. It's like a magic mirror where I see beyond the outward appearance to the heart. I see as God sees. *I see nothing there to pity!* I'm a child of The King, chosen and singled out for His love!

Now I realize that Satan gave me a trick mirror, the kind you see at carnivals and fairs where everything is distorted. In Satan's mirror *I didn't see my real image.*

Some say it's bad luck to break a mirror. But not if it is Satan's!

I crash it to the floor, and it shatters. Everything takes on the festive spirit of a real *Jesus Celebration.* I begin to sing, "Praise God from whom all blessings flow. . . ."

More knocks on my door. Who could that be?

Oh, here are all the people who declined the invitation to my *pity party!*

"May we come in? We heard you're having a *praise party!* That's the kind we *want* to attend!"

Chuck Swindoll said that if you cuddle and nurse self-pity when it is an infant, in a short time it will grow to be a beast, a monster, a raging, coarse brute that will spread the poison of bitterness and paranoia throughout your system. He said that Satan is always urging us to look inward instead of outward and upward. Self-pity is the smog that pollutes the atmosphere and obscures the light of the Son.

Down Memory Lane

A little ways along *Adjustment Avenue* you can turn right at a corner and go down *Memory Lane*. One side of the lane is shady and the other side is bright. The best place to walk is right down the middle of the road.

Feelings of sadness come and go. I continue to have poignant moments and memory flashes. Immediately after Ted's death, memories were fresh, vivid and constant. As time went on, they didn't disrupt my life as much as they did earlier, and I didn't get my primary joy from strolling down Memory Lane.

However, I still need to work through my "no more" thoughts: No more ministry trips to China together. No more cutting his hair, as I had done for 45 years. I would not set a second place at the table. No more relaxing together on the deck outdoors after dinner watching the sunset over the woodland and counting the first evening stars. No more after-dinner walks in the cool of the evening on our subdivision road or leisurely supermarket shopping together, which my husband had such fun doing since his retirement.

No more hearing his characteristic answer when I was on the other end of the phone. No more private high-pitched whistle in a crowd—Ted's signal to locate me—which he taught me to listen for even before we were married.

Hearing a favorite song, being with special people, enjoying some favorite food—these still draw me down Memory Lane but not in black mourning clothes.

I lived many yesterdays with Ted. In fact, I spent *most of my life* with him. My past is inextricably bound with his life. My mind naturally drifts backward to how things used to be, what we did, where we went, what we shared—all are in the past tense. I doubt that the Lord wants me to build a house on Memory Lane and settle there for the rest of my life. Someone wisely advised, *Don't fall over what's behind you.*

Memories are healthy if I occasionally dip back into the past to praise God, but I shouldn't get stuck in the potholes of Memory Lane. How can I rein in my mind from constantly galloping backward? By "bringing every thought into captivity to the mind of Christ" (2 Corinthians 10:5). I am solely responsible for capturing my mind and guiding its thoughts. God won't do that for me. I can direct my thoughts where to go and where not to go.

I'm not at the mercy of my mind. God will give me the strength to lasso my memories and keep them in His corral.

I believe God wants us to gently close the door to the past. By His enabling, we can take our time and savor each memory with sweet sadness, then lay it aside and determine to move on. "One thing I do: forgetting what lies behind and reaching forward to what lies ahead, I press on toward the goal for the prize of the upward call of God in Christ Jesus" (Philippians 4:13,14).

They say old memories are sweet. Well, some of them are, but not all. Let's be real. Some are tinged with less than pleasant times. Sometimes and at some stages of marriage even couples who are devoted to each other have conflicts, difficult interpersonal adjustments, controversies and disagreements. Most of us recall words and actions we now regret. Marriage is not life on fantasy island.

Whatever memories, good or bad, sweet, bitter or mixed, let us lay them at the foot of the Cross. Take them to the Lord and leave them there, neither magnifying nor diminishing them. The past is over.

With eager joy, let's turn a corner and anticipate what God has in store for us. *It's time to make new memories.*

> [The time will come when we should]
> do something different,
> Not too different.
> Just the right amount of difference
> To build a new memory or two.
> Buy a new picture,
> Or learn to paint one.
> Read a new book,
> Or start to write one.
> Take a trip,
> Or at least plan to.
> Read a Psalm-a-day
> And mark your favorite verse.
> When the time is just right—
> do something different! [3]

Aloneness

Early into my singled out life, I felt actual physical discomfort in the pit of my stomach from my new aloneness. I was accustomed to Ted's companionship. We talked things over. We felt warmth in each other's presence even when we were silent. He was there when I came home, and I welcomed him when he returned. We ate together, worked together, loved each other. Now I must live alone.

A dictionary of terms used in publishing and typesetting defines the term "widow." "A very short word, or part of a word, *standing alone* on the last line of a paragraph of body type." I feel like that—I was once part of somebody, but I'm now standing alone as if I were on the last line of some page. I struggle with my aloneness.

There might be a shade of difference between the words alone, lonely and lonesome. Someone said, "Lonesome is when somebody is not there, and you know they will be back after a while. Lonely is when you don't have anybody to be lonesome for." Everyone experiences the emotion of loneliness sometimes. Loneliness isn't selective. It disregards one's status, wealth, even the number of friends. Loneliness can result from the absence of personal intimacy or meaningful activity.

Solitude, on the other hand, is simply being alone, physical separation, not being in the company of others at the moment. It is often positive and renewing. Being alone is essential for the cultivation of the inner spiritual life without which it will lack depth and freshness. We need to be alone to discover and confront our real selves. In a very close marriage where nearly everything is done together, partners may be missing the benefits of such aloneness.

Loneliness is a normal response about which we should not feel guilty because God created us with the need for others of our kind. "Then the Lord God said, 'It is not good for the man to be alone; I will make him a helper suitable for him'" (Genesis 2:18).

God created humankind with a twofold
need: for fellowship with Himself and
companionship with others. When the
link between a married couple is broken
by death, the need for some measure of
coupling with others is important.

"God sets the solitary in families" (Psalm 68:6).
Some versions translate solitary as "lonely." Some widows don't have families. My singled out friend, Brenda,
and her minister husband Ken, never had children. Both
sets of parents died long before her husband did, and
neither Brenda nor Ken had brothers or sisters. Brenda
found a healthy measure of emotional coupling with
other families, with her church family, her neighborhood
and through community service. Nieces and nephews
were part of her concern. Because she is an outgoing, joy-
to-be-around woman in her late seventies, she doesn't
mind being a fifth wheel at events for couples where they
warmly welcome, nurture and care for her. She, in turn,
reaches out to others and cares for them. In that sense,
she is part of many families and no longer solitary.

Twice losing a beloved wife, and after 17 years as
a widower, internationally known missionary, author
and speaker, J. Oswald Sanders, an octogenarian at the
time, shared the following counsel:

The resources available to lonely people, both from God and from fellow men and women, are more abundant than they realize and would discover if they made the attempt. Their loneliness could be the starting point of a new journey toward moral and spiritual maturity.

If they would abandon the search for someone to care for them, and set themselves instead to care for someone else, they would be amazed to discover that their loneliness was quite bearable, even if it was not entirely banished.[4]

Those of us who have families are truly blessed and rich in relationships. Nevertheless, even in our loneliest moment, in our darkest hour, God is there. "I am with you always, to the very end of the age" (Matthew 28:20). We might interpret that as meaning not only to the end of earth's time, but to the end of our lifetime-age.

Always

Is there *no one*
who won't leave me
ever?
Is there *anyone*
who will *never* turn off the light
when I fear the dark?
Is there *someone*
who will respond to my distress
anytime?
Is there One
who will wipe my tears
and truly understand
always?

All arms of flesh may fail.
None can enter completely
into the depths of my being
to be touched
with my infirmity
except my unfailing Lord
who took upon Himself
the form and limitations
of humanity
with passions, emotions
and frailty
of mortality
yet remained immortal
invincible, Divine
so He could care for me
intensively
consistently
in my times of need
always![5]

A friend wrote, "I'm praying that you may become aware more than ever that you are not alone. Our Father truly is the most dependable Companion. Remember, to live alone doesn't mean that you are alone." Another sent me an excerpt from a daily devotional booklet:

There are positive aspects to loneliness. This valley experience foretells the existence of a mountain experience just ahead, for you can't have a valley without a mountain. Loneliness is often the "seed bed of creativity."

This is a new thought for me. I wonder if the next time I am lonely I can remember to ask

God to help me see it as a time for gathering materials for creating something—a pie, a poem, a story, a conversation, a friendship—an extension of myself toward some other person? This will reduce my own loneliness and may contribute toward lifting the burden of aloneness from someone else.[6]

In the days right after Ted died, I seemed too wrapped up in the immediacy of my own circumstances to reach out to others. Nevertheless, before long I recognized that reaching out was the key to my adjustment. Now it is a delight and often a surprise to discover the creativity of aloneness.

The stillness thing

In the early weeks after my husband's death, I had to deal with the unfamiliar stillness that lay heavy in the pit of my stomach. My ears strained for something to break the silence. Was this enforced quiet my enemy, or could it become my friend? Must it leave me in the shadows, or could the sunlight dispel it?

God, are you here in my stillness? In times past You revealed Yourself by a still, small voice. Jesus, You stilled the storm on the Sea of Galilee. You are stilling my life storm with Your "Peace! Be still!" The waves and sea of my inner turmoil need to hear your command: "Be still and know that I am God. The Lord Almighty is with us; the God of Jacob is our fortress" (Psalm 46:10 NIV).

Silence

The house is quiet
with an unaccustomed hush.
I never knew that the clock
ticked so loudly. I listen
intently
to hear
. . . what?
No familiar voice
no happy daily noises
. . . only silence.

No, I *don't* feel him near
for he is *not* here
his chair is empty
his glasses laid aside
his books unread.
The things we did together
I now do alone
I laugh alone
I cry alone
I learn to live alone.

But he hasn't simply vanished . . .
he is elsewhere
more alive than ever
savoring his exciting new state
experiencing endless life and joy!
It is I
who am left behind
alone
for a while.

Then in the stillness
in the mute silence
I hear God whisper
"Not alone . . .
Lo, I am with you always."

Now the silence
becomes my special friend
and I can move on . . . [7]

In the night seasons

We stumble more easily in the dark. If we're walking on a road at night, we can't see the potholes. Nights are worse than other times for me. I hear noises—the creaking house, the whisper of wind and other frightening, imagined sounds. My mind and emotions are exposed, unprotected. Sometimes I wet my pillow with tears. Molehill problems mushroom into gigantic mountains. I wouldn't dare think about *big* problems, or I would never get any sleep. My physical weaknesses are magnified in the darkness.

At night I think of death. Sleep is so much like death. Before my loss, I always kept death at arm's length. I wasn't with my dad when he died suddenly. I was literally an ocean away. Nor was I present at my mother's death, although I was with her during her previous months of hospitalization.

Now death invaded my home, and my husband is gone. We talked about death and what was beyond, but not much about the dying process. The utter finality chills me. Because Ted died in his sleep, I feel more vulnerable at night. I lie awake wondering if *my* heart palpitation is normal. In the first months, I was afraid to stay awake, and afraid to fall asleep. The child's prayer, "If I should die before I wake. . . ." became frighteningly real.

I keep remembering that my husband died alone. Because I live by myself now, panic sometimes grips me when I think that *I* might become ill, need help, cry out and no one will hear me. I, too, could die alone.

I long for the first rays of dawn. The hands of the clock don't seem to move. Yet I'm afraid of the dawn because it brings another day for me to cope with the real world by myself.

When I can't sleep, my imagination works overtime. On the TV screen of my mind I try to enjoy pleasant memory reruns and avoid unpleasant ones. Still, I find myself flipping the channel and displaying the uncertain future over and over.

I borrow tomorrow so I can re-
hearse it and be prepared when it arrives.
I've multiplied its potential terrors a
hundred times. Tomorrow holds
me hostage.

The strange thing about this nightmare is that I must walk through my imagined tomorrow alone—*without God.* Why? Because He never promised to give me strength for tomorrow *before* it gets here. "Therefore do not be anxious for tomorrow; for tomorrow will care for itself. Each day has enough trouble of its own" (Matthew

6:34). When tomorrow comes, *but not before,* God's promises *will be there for me* along with His sure presence. "As thy days, so shall thy strength be" (Deuteronomy 33:25). "My grace is sufficient for you" (2 Corinthians 12:9). That is a present tense promise. I have no business sprinting ahead by imagination to make a "dry run" through tomorrow. The Lord's explicit promise is, *"I will go before you* and make the rough places smooth" (Isaiah 45:2). *God* will go before—but *I'm* not supposed to.

Why do I find it so hard to live one day at a time? God has given me small portions called days because that's all I can manage. When I savor each day slowly, it nourishes me to face the future.

I need enough sleep, but not too much. If I get more than my body and mind need, if I use sleep to escape reality, I become tired and sluggish the next day.

When I'm in the throes of insomnia, rather than thrashing around restlessly in bed, I get up and read or write my thoughts or feelings in a journal. I find it best to use my bed only for sleeping and confine reading to my favorite chair.

I've discovered a way to combat my sleep problem. I take a bulldog grip on one of God's promises. I repeat it mentally over and over before going to sleep, during interrupted sleep or when I awaken too early. It may be a whole verse, a phrase or the words of a hymn. Repetition impresses it indelibly on my spirit, mind and emotions and lulls me to sleep.

"In peace I will both lie down and sleep, for Thou alone, O Lord, dost make me to dwell in safety" (Psalm 4:8). What a comfort to fall asleep in God's "safety zone!"

Before I go to bed I like to think about
some reason to get up in the morning. If
I plan one enjoyable thing to do tomorrow, I can drift off to sleep with the motivation of anticipation.

I know I'm going to make it. I have coping power
within me, but not in the sense of my human potential.
I internalize the truth that *Christ is actually within me,*
the One who said all power was given to Him in heaven
and on earth. (Matthew 28:18) Jesus is my strength for
the hours of darkness. He is sufficient for the dawn and
the new day. "God is within her, she will not fall. God will
help her at break of day" (Psalm 46:5).

*Lord, I'm Your restless sheep. Settle me down in
peace in Your fold for the night. I trust You because You
declared, "I am The Door." Thank you for Your Holy
Spirit who is the security guard at my heart's door.*

*When tomorrow dawns, You will be there, Lord,
waiting at its door to help me leap over all the potholes on
Adjustment Avenue.*

A book on grief suggested,
"Being widowed turns your self-
image upside down. You feel dizzy,
off-center, without direction. You
need to reset your compass."
However, if your compass as a
Christian woman has been pointing
to Jesus as Lord throughout your
life, you don't need to buy
a new compass.

Resetting My Compass

An immediate feeling of disorientation, the ambiguity of a new role and the finality of separation from a spouse are intensely real to a new widow. However, what we are going through now should not throw us off center. We are never out of God's care and love. If our compass always pointed to Jesus Christ as the Lord of our lives, *we don't need a new compass*. We only need to keep our new lives aligned in God's direction day by day. Our widowhood did not take God by surprise. It was part of His perfect, sovereign plan for us.

Nursery of my grief

I hope we are now convinced that we shouldn't skip our grieving process because it is our teacher and necessary for our transition. It should last a reasonable time, long enough for our adjustment. Long grieving doesn't mean we loved our husband more. Likewise, if we are ready to move on without him, that we loved him less.

Too short a time spent in the grieving process diminishes its positive aspects. To try returning to "normal" too quickly may not be healthy. To stay *too long* is also counterproductive. We should not wallow in grief. I could easily become morbid and brooding. I've seen its deteriorating effects on some of my widow and widower friends who continued to grieve too long.

Working through grief is a *forward movement*. We shouldn't stay submerged in our sadness. If we drag our feet, we may get stuck in wet cement. Grieving can become too comfortable and familiar. We embrace it, and may not want to look for God's new assignment. It's easier to continue in a predictable mode. Each of us must achieve her own balance between the two extremes.

The day will come when I realize I have been focusing too long on my emotional loss, my hurts, wounds and singleness. I've been thinking of myself as handicapped. Yet to others, especially to strangers or in public, *I don't look any different—certainly not disabled*. Widowhood is not a badge to wear so that everyone will recognize my new identity. I haven't changed on the outside since my husband left for heaven.

Early in my new role, I caught myself drifting toward "the widows' pews" at church. As a new single again, I stood at the back of the church shouting (inwardly!) at everyone, "Look at me! I'm a widow. I'm alone. Pity me. Befriend me!"

At first I thought about attending a widows' support group in my community. That may be very helpful to some, but not necessarily to everyone. It is a temporary reinforcement while my brokenness mends, but it should not become a permanent crutch.

Working through my feelings, I found it healthier to mainstream myself even from the earliest days. The loss of my husband doesn't change who I am. Marriage is only part of life's many relationships.

I shouldn't look at myself as different from "regular" people. My real disability is my own attitude, which isn't visible. It is, however, expressed by my actions. I want people to see *the person I am,* not the loss I've suffered.

Jesus' instruction to those who fast might also apply to us as singled out women. He said that those who fast shouldn't advertise what they are doing by their outward appearance. They should wash their faces and act "normal." When I look and act as if I'm grieving, for whose benefit is my performance? What is my motive?

I don't *impress my departed husband* with my love and loyalty by making a spectacle of my grief. My time for expressing love and loyalty to him is over.

I don't *impress God* with my outward show of grief, nor earn any "Brownie points" with Him.

If I continue in excessive or prolonged grief, what am I *showing others?* That I don't agree with God's decision in my life? That I miss my husband? Of course I miss him. However, shouldn't that be a private matter for me to deal with, to adjust to, to move on through with God's help? If I continue displaying a sad face, I obviously want to attract pity. The first impression people will have of me is that I am grieving.

I have not lost my worth to God or to people. I have only lost my husband, my partner, my mate. I was a person of worth before I met him. We united our lives for many years. Without him I'm still a person of worth. I haven't lost my individual personhood.

I have truly lost a significant part of me because we were one, but we were also two and separate before we married. I'm still intact! I'm spiritually whole, not fractured. I have a wound, but it will heal. If I keep the wound fresh with sustained expressions of grief, it won't heal.

We've established the biblical view that our loyalty to our husbands ends at their death. That's simply a fact, not a hardhearted judgment. My love for my husband and my memories do not stop. The time comes when I must move out of the comfort of the nursery of my grieving and enter the race course of life again.

When death takes your special person,
it hurts.
But it hurts a little less with time
and still less with more time.
How much time?
More for some
and less for others.
There is no prescribed amount for recovery.

But one morning you will wake up and your loss
will not be the first thing you think about.
Then you will know
that it's just a little better
than it was in the beginning.

Time does help!
Let God comfort and strengthen you
through His Word.

When death takes your special person,
give yourself some time,
just the right amount of time for you.
Not too little,
and not too much.[1]

Rebuilding self-confidence

My cousin, Martha, sent us a gift box of 1,000 fancy return address labels just before my husband suddenly changed his address to heaven. They were *Mr. and Mrs.* labels. I kept using them because I didn't want to waste them, and I didn't have any with only my name. For months I simply crossed out Ted's name.

This became a psychological downer. It reminded me that I was the leftover half of a couple. I had to move on as a person in my own right before the Lord and before others.

I decided to become a big spender and ordered rainbow-colored, gummed address labels with only my name for the grand sum of $2.99 plus tax! I omitted the *Mrs.* prefixing my name.

Eventually I have come to accept that the "we" part of our marriage is over. I can no longer expect mutual decision making. Some had husbands who made most of the decisions, and now they find it difficult to trust their own. We may lack self-confidence and can't seem to get our self-esteem in gear. If we look at ourselves as useless "leftover" persons without our husbands, we're prime candidates for feelings of inadequacy. As Christians, however, we don't have to rebuild our self-esteem from scratch.

A book on grief suggested, "Realize that self-confidence comes from *within* you." That's only partly true. As Christians, we believe that self-confidence comes from outside us, from confidence in God. It is Christ living in us who gives true confidence.

Early in my widowhood, I often had a slip of the tongue and referred to myself as "we." With effort, I eventually changed to "I" but not a lonely, bereft "I." Rather, an "I" that stands up straight and tall, confident that I am "singled out" for *God's special attention.*

Some secular books on grief suggest that I should fake self-confidence, proclaim that I'm the greatest, that I can do anything. In affirming that, they claim, I will begin to feel it. I am supposed to talk myself into confidence. Again, a core of truth is there, but the basis of that advice is humanistic, rooted in self-effort and self-sufficiency.

As a Christian, I don't need to fake it. "With Him [Christ] all things are possible." "I can do all things through Christ who strengthens me." "Be not afraid of their faces; be courageous," God's Word declares. God promises to give me strength and courage when I step out on His promises. That is entirely different from playacting. *We declare God's truth,* as in the chorus:

> Give thanks with a grateful heart,
> give thanks to the Holy One;
> Give thanks because He's given
> Jesus Christ His Son.
> And now let the weak say, "I am strong,"
> Let the poor say, "I am rich"
> because of what the Lord has done for us!

Because God *has given me His Son* who *is* my wisdom, strength and courage, I can face a singled out life. God doesn't merely *give* those things—He *is* the personification of them. Having Him, I *experience* His sufficiency. I don't have to talk myself into self-confidence.

Are we having fun yet?

To some who are watching our behavior as singled out women it may seem sacrilegious when we start to laugh and appear happy. Or at least disrespectful, somehow disloyal to the departed spouse. For us who know where our spouse is, the reality of his presence with Jesus, the question of disrespect or disloyalty doesn't enter in. Our spouse is "having fun" in the deepest, liberated sense of the word. He is enjoying himself. No tears, no pain, no physical limitations. He is discovering what incredible beauty and delights God has prepared for His children in their new immortal state. Would Ted be unhappy if he knew I was moving on and finding joy in life under the care of the Lord? I don't believe so.

It's O.K. for me to be happy and enjoy
life, to make new friends, to celebrate life
for as long as the Lord lends me breath.

I think that neither my husband nor the Lord would want me to waste an inordinate amount of time sorrowing instead of redeeming the time. One singled out friend said, "One day I laughed. Sometime later I found myself humming. Then I sang." Joy will come.

If we want to be strong for our new assignment, it's not only permissible but essential to experience the joy of the Lord. The Bible says "Do not be grieved, for the joy of the Lord is your strength" (Nehemiah 8:10). I need all the strength I can get.

"I will rejoice in You and be in high spirits; I will sing praise to Your name, O Most High!" (Psalm 9:2) If I am moving on to greater intimacy with the Lord, as I should be, I will be rejoicing in the Lord for His goodness. Not to do so would be contrary to His revealed will. "Rejoice always" (1 Thessalonians 5:16). *Always* means in whatever circumstances I find myself *today.*

Acceptance of my situation is only the first step toward adjustment. Step two is *joy.* In various versions of the Bible, Romans 5:3 is translated "glory in tribulations," "glory in afflictions," "rejoice when we run into problems," "rejoice in our sufferings," "exult in our tribulations," "boast of our troubles." The Amplified version even extends the meaning: "Let us also be full of joy now! Let us exult and triumph in our troubles and rejoice in our sufferings."

James 1:2 echoes: "Consider yourselves fortunate when all kinds of trials come your way," "count it all joy," "consider it complete joy," "then be happy." The Amplified again gives me tasty dessert to linger over: "Consider it wholly joyful, my brethren, whenever you are enveloped in or encounter trials of any sort, or fall into various temptations."

In Matthew 5:12 Jesus puts His own seal on the response He expects from me when I meet trials of any kind: "Rejoice and be exceeding glad," "be glad and supremely joyful," "Be happy about it! Be very glad!"

The whole prospect is the exact opposite of my *natural* inclination after the loss of my husband. That's because it is a *supernatural* response which I must receive from the Lord.

Rejoicing . . . even if?

Writing 600 years before Christ and faced with devastating catastrophes, the prophet Habakkuk used terms similar to the New Testament passages above. His whole world, personal and national, was in ruins. The economy was in shambles, and the national leadership was weak.

Read his *state-of-the-heart* testimony:

> Though the fig tree should not blossom, and there be no fruit on the vines; though the yield of the olive should fail, and the fields produce no food; though the flock should be cut off from the fold, and there be no cattle in the stalls, *yet* I will exult in the Lord, I will rejoice in the God of my salvation. (Habakkuk 3:17)

The context suggests that Habakkuk was whooping it up, celebrating, making merry in a boisterous party fashion. The Hebrew word for "exulting" means to leap for joy and spin around in the presence of God, to rejoice exceedingly, be highly elated or jubilant. Habakkuk was celebrating *because the Lord God was his strength!* His joy in life didn't depend on any material things or his own well-being. He anchored his joy in His God.

Does God expect a similar response from me under my present circumstances? Instead of grieving in the world's fashion, can I join Habakkuk on the chorus of that joyful song?

> Yet will I rejoice in the Lord, I will exult in the [victorious] God of my salvation! The Lord is my strength, my personal bravery *and*

my invincible army; He makes my feet like hind's feet, and will make me to walk [not to stand still in terror, but to walk] and make [spiritual] progress upon my high places [of trouble, suffering or responsibility]! (Habakkuk. 3:18,19 Amplified)

Since God is my salvation and strength, He wants to lead me beyond the "grin and bear it" level. He wants to teach me how to make *joyful spiritual progress* out of my personal loss. How can I apply Habakkuk's "even ifs" to my own situation?

Even if everything around me has changed since the death of my husband, even if I am in financially difficult straits, even if my loneliness is more than I can bear, even if I must move from familiar surroundings, even if friends and family are far from me, even if my own health fails, even if my whole world seems upside down and I face an uncertain future . . . yet I will rejoice in the Lord. I will steadfastly hold on to my faith in a good God whom I trust implicitly. I can be highly elated, leaping for joy and spinning around in the presence of God!

I can express such elation in my spirit, and I can even literally leap for joy in private if I want to. *I believe God would be pleased!* If I have the privilege and opportunity of living alone, I enjoy an entirely new kind of liberty. As I sit or walk around in my home and attend to my daily responsibilities, I feel free to talk with the Lord. I thank Him aloud for my many obvious blessings and for His daily provisions.

I don't forget to thank God for the negative things which have *not* happened to me, the things from which I am spared. I can sing and pray and praise without disturbing anyone. No one is around to think I am strange. "I will praise You, O Lord, with my whole heart; I will show forth (recount and tell aloud) all Your marvelous works *and* wonderful deeds!" (Psalm 9:1 Amplified)

I'm trying to practice this positive recounting of God's goodness even for little things I might ordinarily overlook or take for granted. I set my mind to do that. I hope I'm moving closer to what the Bible calls *praying without ceasing.* (1 Thessalonians 5:17)

It's becoming ever more real to me that I'm *not* living alone. The Lord and I live together in this house. *It is His home.* Certainly we will talk together, but in the silent times, as I sit in my recliner for extended periods, *I will do the listening.* I listen for Him to speak to me through His Word, through my thoughts, my impressions and my reading. Since the Holy Spirit dwells in me, I ask for the mind of Christ to be in me.

I'm discovering some wonderful things during those silent times. "And the joy we share as we tarry there, none other has ever known."

Adjusting to life with Christ

When my husband and I lived together, I tried not to intentionally do anything to make him uncomfortable. I respected him and his wishes. I decorated and arranged the rooms of each house in which we lived through the years according to his needs, habits and preferences. Many times I fell short, I'm sure, but I did try to please him. Where I failed, I will have to apply, "I'm not perfect, but forgiven." Ted was not heavy-handed, authoritarian or hard to please. He was happy to let me be creative and follow my desires.

Now that my Lord and I are living alone together, I need to evaluate my life and adjust my activities to His wishes. I should make some changes, shipshape the rooms of my life, rearrange some things to make the Lord feel at home. I need to be sure my spiritual compass points in His direction.

As I meditate and wait on Him, He begins *gently and lovingly*, not harshly, to impress me with areas in my life where I need to run a tighter ship to please Him. He wants me to be a better steward of my time on earth and not fritter it away on the trivial. The Scriptures encourage us to "try to learn what is pleasing to the Lord" (Ephesians 5:10).

I would do well to follow the principles set forth in Philippians 4:8: "Finally, brethren, whatever is true, whatever is honorable, whatever is right, whatever is pure, whatever is lovely, whatever is of good repute, if there is any excellence, and if anything worthy of praise, let your mind dwell on these things."

For instance, I don't feel that the Lord requires me to pull the plug on my TV or haul it off to the junk yard, but the Lord impressed me to apply the above verses more carefully.

I'm responsible to obey in any area of my life He puts His finger on. *Light obeyed, increaseth light; light rejected, bringeth night.* If I don't obey the Holy Spirit's prompting, God's light may grow dimmer in my life. "It is God who works within [me] both to will and to do [work] his pleasure" (Philippians 2:13).

Either I'm a good steward of the 24 hours God gives me each day or a poor one. Does what I do help me to find and fulfill my new assignment from the Lord? What weights so easily beset me that I should lay aside? To eliminate some frivolous activities or time wasters is not the whole picture, however. I need to substitute positive things.

If I've watched TV, for instance, as a mindless filler when I'm tired, I could take a nap instead and then do something more pleasing to the Lord. I could substitute exercise or a walk. I could read some of those books and magazines for which I never seem to have time and thus stretch and enrich my mind. I could dust off my library card and tap into the wealth of books and video tapes. Through reading I can enter into the lives of others, travel to other countries and experience other cultures.

Each singled out friend has different areas of her life to bring into obedience to the Lord. He will let us know what pleases Him, if we take time to listen.

My slice of pie

When a pie is sliced, *portions* are given out. Some people ask for smaller, some for larger portions. Do I covet someone else's slice of life and resent their continuing happily married state? I must search my heart for my true, deep-down feelings.

The Lord is my everlasting portion! Everlasting is not short-lived pleasure. Not temporary like a piece of pie—a few minutes in the mouth and it's gone. The Lord's plan for my days on earth doesn't end but continues in eternity. The Lord has *portioned* the single life to me again. Does this *new portion* bring me closer to Him? Is the Lord truly "more than friend or life to me"?

Do I say "Thank you" and accept my *portion* from

God with joy? Or do I reject it and push His hand away? Do I kick against the pricks and pout about my unfortunate lot in life now that I'm a widow? My new portion is not easy, but what is my alternative?

Whom have I in heaven but Thee? And beside Thee I desire nothing on earth. My flesh and my heart may fail, but God is the strength of my heart and *my portion* forever (Psalm 73:25,26).

The Lord is the *portion* of my inheritance and my cup; Thou dost support my lot. The lines have fallen to me in pleasant places; Indeed, my heritage is beautiful to me (Psalm 16:5,6).

The Lord is my portion (Psalm 119:57).

My Portion

The Lord is my portion.

I don't desire a tastier piece
of life. Or bigger
or smaller. Nor do I covet
my neighbor's plot.
My lot is assigned
by God's design
shaped by love
in His flawless plan.
It doesn't matter
if grass looks greener
elsewhere, meadows more lush
or brooks run swifter, clearer
beyond the fence

that circumscribes
my appointed heritage.

You, Lord, are my portion!
None other do I seek.
And if there is no human arm
on which to lean
no shoulder
to wet with my tears
no one to hug,
help me
to walk my path contentedly
accept my portion joyfully
assenting to Your blueprint
Your good and perfect will
for me *this* day, *each* day
because You *are* The Way
You are my portion, Lord![2]

End of the tunnel

Will we *ever* see the light at the end of the tunnel?
The light that leads us out of the tunnel? Yes, grieving is
a journey with an end!

God designed us with the internal ability to adjust to life's most jarring losses. That
adjustment will not take place in a matter of
days or even weeks if the loss was severe.
Months and years are more realistic. This is not
to say that if a loved one dies that you will not
be able to cope for a very long time, but rather,
that you will be affected and that you will

continue to adjust your inner and outer life for a long time. We instinctively look for ways to cope from the outset, and, with God's grace, we will find ways to make it through long days and sometimes longer nights. But with the passage of time, *the journey will be completed.* Sometimes we take just baby steps, at other times we make longer gains. The completion of the journey does not mean that our memories will be erased.

Even when we approach the end of the journey that does not mean that in future years we will not have a stab of pain when we remember the time of separation when the loss occurred. But we will have learned how to change our lives to a new, adapted, mode of living.[3]

A friend wrote of finally moving on: "At first I felt immobilized. I couldn't do anything except the daily necessities. Sometimes I was afraid I would never come out of it. When caught in my car during a torrential downpour one day, I wrote: *The solid sheets of rain become the womb that holds my aching heart.* Finally, one spring morning, I awoke to the sound of birds singing. I smiled and thought: *even the birds know it's going to get better.*" She wrote:

I've been paralyzed
frozen in time
like a hibernating bear
trapped in a cold season of life.
How I want to awaken
and feel the spring warmth
penetrating my very being

forcing me to action
shaking me from lethargy!
Spring must be approaching:
I feel faint stirrings
my soul wants to leap
but my mind is fuzzy
my body weak;
but it's approaching . . .
Spring *always* comes!"

Permission to get well

Jesus asked the man at the pool in Jerusalem if he wanted to be "made whole." Of course he did—who wouldn't after being "unwhole" for 38 years? The question was appropriate, however.

Some people don't want to get well, some don't want to get over their grief and be "made whole." They are comfortable with the perks of grieving. The time will come when you must decide whether you want to get well. Although time is a great healer of grief, even time doesn't heal automatically. Healing requires an act of your will. The time comes when you need to assume responsibility for your own recovery. You will know when that time comes because you will be ready.

At first you needed to give yourself permission to grieve. Eventually you need to give yourself permission to stop grieving.

Life is not supposed to end with the death of your loved one. You are to grow and never stop growing. New experiences are ahead of you. You have new worlds to explore, new feelings to feel, new relationships to develop. In the process, *a new you* can come forth. A singled out woman admitted, "It is as if I'm another woman now, and I like her better. But it was a hard birth."

"Sweet are the uses of adversity; Which, like the toad, ugly and venomous, Wears yet a precious jewel in its head," wrote William Shakespeare in *As You Like It*. A time of trouble is a time to grow. You may feel that you'll never grow again because you have been cut down. You are like a tree cut off nearly to the ground, separated from the main trunk and foliage when your spouse died.

I saw a remarkable illustration in the well-kept yard of my cousins in heartland Iowa. They had to saw down a large oak tree to within two feet of the ground because of danger to the roof of their house. It looked like the death of that tree. However, the next season, with the warmth of the sun and the nourishment of spring rain, it sprouted a healthy, slim, green branch. Several new leaves reached upward from the side of the stump, within inches of the sawed off portion.

"For there is hope of a tree if it be cut down, that it will sprout again, that the tender branch thereof will not cease" (Job 14:7).

I saw a picture of a huge Douglas fir tree that a storm had uprooted. The tree lay on the ground, its enormous root system exposed to the elements. A small portion of the root, however, remained firmly in the ground and had proved adequate support for continued growth of the huge tree. Apparently years had passed since the original storm, for the picture recorded an amazing thing: That tree trunk, leveled as it was, had indeed begun growing again! [4]

Even after a tree has been felled by natural calamities or by human hands, the inner life force struggles to maintain life from its roots. As a singled out woman, you, too, can keep growing and reaching upward no matter what adversities appear to topple you. If Christ, your Lord, lives within you, your root system is strong enough to sustain you. That includes the apparent crumbling of your world when your spouse died.

The new you will not come easily, nor will it come quickly. First a tender shoot of growth, then a stronger branch. You must crawl before you walk, as a young child does. It's like beginning a new life again, but it will come, if you are willing.

So, let's move on to receive our new assignment! 🐾

I'm teamed with God alone now—an exciting yoke—and I can expect new priorities, goals and strength. Also, new friends, joys and new freedom. Best of all, I can look forward to new spiritual depth in my relationship with the Lord.

9 *Receiving God's Assignment*

New beginnings

New paths are more scary because I don't know what's around the corner. I don't have the companionship and counsel of my husband to bolster my courage.

Within a few days of my loss, a good friend wrote me, "Our Heavenly Father is still in the business of 'making all things new.' Don't be surprised at new supplies, new directions and new relationships on your new road."

My tendency is to look back on the old, the familiar, the comfortable and mourn their loss. Memories are precious. It's good to remember and cherish them, but I must balance the past with the apostle Paul's admonition to press on.

Another friend who has been singled out for her new assignment several decades ago nourished my spirit with her counsel:

> God has something new for us. What? Well, we can wake up each morning anticipating what God is going to do this day. How is He going to use me? God didn't ask us if we wanted to go through bereavement, but He does prom-

ise never to leave us or forsake us. Let's reach up and take His righteous right hand. It is always there to take our fears away. Aren't you thankful He didn't give us a spirit of fear but of power, love and a sound mind? Look for new dimensions God is going to bring into your life and greet them with open arms.

"Forget about becoming your 'old self' again," advised another friend. "Renewed faith in God and in yourself will make you an even better person capable of both loving and living normally again."

Jennie, a pastor's widow, newly singled out after nearly 60 years of marriage, regularly chooses a Scripture verse to send me and prays for me according to its promise. "Yesterday I chose for you," she wrote, "'Eye hath not seen, nor ear heard, neither have entered into the heart of man, the things which God hath prepared for them that love Him. But God hath revealed them unto us by his Spirit'" (1 Corinthians 2:9, 10 KJV).

Yes, Lord! I do love You. Let's get on with the things You have prepared for me.

You and I have processed our grief, accepted our present state and are moving forward to adjustment—all under the Lordship of Jesus Christ. Now we reach for our future.

The Lord promised to secure both my *future* and my *past*. "For the Lord will go *before* you, and the God of Israel will be your *rear* guard" (Isaiah 52:12). Isaiah 58:8 restates that promise, "The glory of the Lord will be your rear guard." I progress in my adjustment when I focus not on what is behind—the death of my spouse—but what is ahead. My past life is over and locked in God's care. He keeps the key and will guard it until I stand before Him.

"One thing I do: forgetting what lies behind and reaching forward to what lies ahead, I press on toward the goal for the prize of the upward call of God in Christ Jesus" (Philippians 3:13,14).

For the rest of my time on earth God leads me *forward* and goes before me, drawing me on in the direction He wants me to go. He is there before I get there. Because He lives I can face tomorrow.

The Lord was with me from birth, He was there during my married life, and He is with me since my married life is over. As important as my marriage was, it was still *only an interval* in God's lifelong and eternity-long plan for me. "I am Alpha and Omega, the first and the last" (Revelation 1:11). God takes care of me over a lifetime. "Surely goodness and lovingkindness will follow me *all the days of my life*" (Psalm 23:6).

When we started on this journey together, I suggested that we shouldn't consider ourselves widows for the rest of our lives. Widowhood still connects us to our marriage, which is over. Widowhood is not a rut to get stuck in and never get out. It is a tunnel from which we emerge, only a transition, a temporary period *to pass through* on the way to healthy *single personhood*.

Eventually, in the time that best suits each of us, we should come out of the widowhood tunnel to walk in the sunshine of God's life assignment for the rest of our days.

Why am I left behind?

One of the possible first reactions to my husband's death is to ask, "Why am I left behind?" If it represents a pouting complaint with self-pity overtones directed to no one in particular, the question doesn't require an answer. However, as an *honest inquiry* to our Heavenly Father, He probably would answer, "I'm glad you asked." He will eagerly reveal it to each of us. Probably not all at once but day by day because we can only understand it in small portions. I may not fully know in this life what my assignment was, but God will show me enough of it so I can carry it out under His guidance. Yes, even without knowing His big picture.

Apparently I still have some life classroom time ahead of me, brief or long, because the Lord has left me on earth for now.

Although my husband and I were united on our earthly journey, in God's view we each had a separate curriculum and assignments. God had one life purpose for my husband, another for me. My husband finished his, but I still have my course to complete.

I am God's workmanship independent of my husband. My assignment has been prepared even before I was married. *God promised to accomplish all things for me, too, and He's going to finish that good work through me.* "For I am confident of this very thing, that He who began a good work in you will perfect it until the day of Christ Jesus" (Philippians 1:6).

I don't want to abort God's personal plan for me by considering my life assignment over just because my husband died. This is no time to give up and coast to my personal finish line. In the words of a gospel song, "I want to run the last mile home." I want to run the race on God's track with my eyes on *His goal for me*.

From his own experience recorded in the first chapter of Philippians, Paul provides a clue about why I am left behind: "But if I am to live on in the flesh, this will mean fruitful labor for me." Not to pursue self interest, but to be productive in witness and service. Verses 24 to 26 define our assignment in respect to those who benefit from our labor: "...for *your* sake... for *your* progress and joy in the faith ... through my coming to *you* again."

As singled out Christian women, part of the reason we are left behind is to be spiritually productive *in our relationships*. We are here for the benefit of others, to encourage them in the faith. That is an assignment for which you and I really need our Teacher's help!

Among the survivors

So far, I'm a survivor. Beverly, a singled out survivor described her feelings vividly:

> How did I learn I was a "survivor?" It was in the newspaper. My husband's obituary read: "He is survived by his wife, Beverly, of the home."
>
> I didn't want to survive. I wanted to die too. Death had to be easier than surviving! *Surviving!* I learned to survive. I survived the sleepless nights, tortured days, endless weeks, holidays, Sundays, months of hopelessness. Survival of the fittest—I became strong. I did survive. Amazingly, now I'm proud to be a survivor. I deserve a medal for the battle scars. [1]

I'm still a player on the stage of life. Having faced death, how keenly I now realize that every breath is under God's control. I'm literally just a heartbeat away from finishing my course. Acts 17:28 reminds me that "in Him we live and move and exist."

Am I alive today just because I'm a tough customer or have a good genetic makeup? Am I simply hanging on and marking time until my number is up?

As a Christian, I can be sure God's special plan has kept me alive until this moment. It was not by my own will or my healthy lifestyle, nourishing food, or the skill of medical science that I have lived to see this dawn.

God doesn't keep it a secret why He extends the life of any Christian. I'm living today to *be* what He wants me to *be*, to *do* what He wants me to *do*, to *speak* what He wants me to *say* in witness for Him. God created me *to praise Him and have fellowship with Him.* Isaiah 43:21 declares, "The people *whom I formed for Myself* will declare My praise."

The Westminster Catechism asks, "What is the chief end [purpose] of man?" The answer, "Man's chief end is to glorify God and enjoy Him forever." That means now, during my life on earth, not only after I'm in heaven.

What an honor! What a privilege!

A new assignment?

"In the year of King Uzziah's death, I saw the Lord sitting on a throne, lofty and exalted" (Isaiah 6:1). From an introductory note to the book of Isaiah, the writer explains: "Isaiah may have had a ministry before, but he tagged the death of the King as the time when he received a special anointing and commission from God." Isaiah made himself available when the Lord asked whom He should send and "who will go for Us?"

Shouldn't I expect a new commission and a special anointing from God in the year (or whatever span of time) after my husband died? Have I seen the Lord in a new way, "high and lifted up," sovereign in all His ways, carrying out His plan in my life? Have I made myself available to the Lord instead of being overly concerned with my loss and preoccupied with "working through my grief"?

When I realize how suddenly one can cross the finish line of life and how quickly time can run out, I see the urgency of getting on with my personal agenda. I should relentlessly pursue, with whatever measure of strength God gives me, my individual assignment from the Lord. Each of us singled out women needs to look to the Lord for that personal assignment.

Must my assignment be *new*? No, the Lord might want me to continue an assignment that He gave me when I was still part of a couple. I can carry on some things alone that were done with my husband before.

The Lord might want to give me an entirely new assignment for which I may need further training. The Lord might even reassign me to something I did before I was married. Or any combination of the above.

We shouldn't think of our assignment as some big

deal, something for which we need to get dressed up and travel somewhere else to perform. Nor something we need to stand on a platform to deliver.

Above all, let's *not compare our assignment* from the Lord with someone else's. God deals with each of us where we are, knowing what we are, our abilities, limitations and opportunities. He only expects us to be all *we* can be for Him. By our obvious life of joyfully trusting the Lord, we can be faithful witnesses to His keeping power and sufficiency.

Our assignment may simply mean living a lifestyle to please Jesus Christ as Lord of our lives. We can bloom gently and quietly where we are.

The third verse of the hymn, "May the Mind of Christ, My Savior" may describe our assignment: "May the peace of God, my Father, rule my life in everything, that I may be calm *to comfort sick and sorrowing.*"

Habitats for eternity

Whatever other specific assignment the Lord gives us, we singled out Christian women should go into the building business. Not literal construction work like "Habitats for Humanity," building housing facilities for the needy. Good as they are, those dwellings will pass away.

We should be more concerned with "Habitats for Eternity." The houses we help to build by exhortation and encouragement are the lives of other Christians.

> We have a building from God, an eternal house in heaven, not built by human hands. . . . longing to be clothed with our heavenly dwelling (2 Corinthians 5:1,2 NIV).
> Therefore encourage one another and build each other up, just as in fact you are doing (1 Thessalonians 5:11 NIV).
> Therefore encourage each other with these words [about the coming of Christ for His Church] (1 Thessalonians 4:18 NIV).
> [Speak] only what is helpful for building others up according to their needs, that it may benefit those who listen (Ephesians 4:29 NIV).

Without doubt, this building up of one another is pleasing to the Lord. It is one answer to our sincere question, "Why am I left behind?"

> Blessed be the God and Father of our Lord Jesus Christ, the Father of mercies and God of all comfort: who comforts us in all our affliction so that we may be able to comfort those who are in any affliction with the comfort with which we ourselves are comforted by God.
> For just as the sufferings of Christ are ours in abundance, so also our comfort is abundant through Christ. But if we are afflicted, it is for your comfort and salvation; or if we are comforted, it is for your comfort (2 Corinthians 1:3-6).

As God has seen us through our loss, so He wants us to hold the hands of our singled out sisters, especially those newly joining our ranks. Let's reach out to them early in their grieving process when they need our tender but strong support.

Let's be sure to be there for them as the days and months go by "when other helpers fail and comforts cease," as the hymn writer so aptly observes. *Our most important assignment* may be to quietly, faithfully invest our lives in others.

> One reason we suffer is to be prepared to bring encouragement and comfort to others who come across our path enduring a similar situation. Remember that! Look back at the chain reaction: We suffer . . . God comes alongside to comfort . . . others suffer . . . we step alongside to comfort them. With God's arm firmly around my shoulders, I have the strength and stability to place my arm around the shoulder of another. Isn't this true? Similar experiences create mutual understanding.
>
> Because of this, we can confidently say that our troubling circumstances are *never* in vain. The bruises may hurt, but they are not without reason. God is uniquely preparing us for the comfort others will need. In one sense, we are all "preparing for the ministry." Our Father is preparing us to meet the deep inner needs of others by bringing us through the dark places first. [2]

Don't waste your sorrows

We don't have to wait until we've victoriously and completely adjusted to our new single life before we comfort and encourage others. Several book titles speak to our new circumstances: "Don't Waste Your Sorrows," "Turn It Into Gold," "Turn It Into Glory." We should maximize our learning experience for the benefit of others.

In the first year after my husband died, six friends and acquaintances also lost their husbands. We were all vulnerable, needy and sensitively open to the Lord's gentle shepherding.

I couldn't afford to wait until I had every-thing "together" myself. We struggled together, comforted one another, prayed for each other, hugged and learned as we went along.

Since I've been on the receiving end of comfort, I'm more conscious of some right and wrong things that would-be comforters say to the grieving—the wise and perhaps unwise things. Nevertheless, a singled out friend told me she would still rather have someone make a genuine effort to comfort her and express the "wrong" sentiments than not come or call at all.

Another said she was most nourished and comforted by those who came but said little. "They were just there. I appreciated friends who came silently alongside and let me talk if I wanted to. I welcomed those who didn't probe if I was silent, who affirmed my feelings and didn't tell me how I should or should not be feeling."

During Job's time of intense suffering, some of his friends sat silently with him seven days and nights before they said anything. From what they said afterward, perhaps they would have done better to *remain* quiet! They gave Job more comfort during those silent days. There is a time for silence and a time to speak.

The friends I appreciated most were good listeners. If part of my new assignment is to encourage other singled out women, I want to be that kind of friend. I've learned that it's all right to talk about our spouses and share memories. It's natural to refer to our spouses by name and recall tender or even humorous incidents about their lives. A real friend always takes her cue from her grieving friend.

It is healthful and freeing to talk about our husband's death because, as we go over the details, it helps us face reality. It's not morbid but normal to relive any crisis experience. We each need to make our own way through the maze of unfamiliar feelings and at our own pace. Of course, I still don't have all the answers, but I hope I'm progressing and learning.

Sondra, my professional grief counselor friend, said that her professor cautioned her never to say, "I know just how you feel." Even if one *has* experienced the same or similar loss, another's emotions and coping attempts may be quite different. In her counselor training sessions quite a list of "nevers" was given. Although the statements may be true, it's probably not wise to say, "You'll get over it." Or "It could have been worse." Or "At least you're alive." Or "You're young, you'll marry again." Especially we should not say, "Call me if you need me." How I wished those who said that to me had called *me*— often and regularly, even occasionally. Most of us feel embarrassed and awkward to hold such well-intentioned people to their polite, offhand offers.

I want to be a good friend who doesn't try to prove

anything. I want to be a representative of the Great Comforter, to love my hurting friends, touch them, if appropriate, weep with them, show them the compassion of Jesus through my own compassion.

Many people are uncomfortable or embarrassed talking to the bereaved. Perhaps our presence reminds them of their own mortality or the possibility of losing their spouse. Couples may seem to avoid us. Do they think we are bad luck or something? A good rule of thumb is to give would-be comforters the benefit of the doubt—learn to accept them as they are, and not as we would like them to be.

Before I went through the experience of loss myself, I felt extremely uncomfortable around the bereaved. I sincerely wanted to help, but because I didn't know what to do or say, I avoided them.

I was "all thumbs" when trying to console others who were hurting, going through surgeries, cancer, loss of a mate—and aging. I did reach out my arms but they seemed too short. When I hugged hurting people, I didn't feel that my embrace was warm enough.

Then the Lord brought me through all the above experiences, and I began to learn what compassion really was. God gave me longer arms to reach around others and embrace them to my heart. I hope I'm more patient with others who try to be kind but may be clumsy in their consoling.

The questions and comments of most people are well-meaning, though possibly inappropriate sometimes. They usually stem from inexperience. After I was well along in my adjustment, I started to keep a list of awkward comments people made (which I won't show anyone). Eventually they struck me as amusing, though well-intentioned.

Nothing in my house?

I may think I have "nothing in my house." Nothing in my earthly storehouse of talents, skills, gifts, possessions, abilities, training or opportunities with which to pursue and fulfill any assignment the Lord gives me. Let's look at a widow who had much less than any of us. Second Kings 4:1-7 records the story.

A godly man "from the company of the prophets" died. He had been a man who "feared the Lord." His widow was hard pressed for daily necessities and apparently was left with minor children still living at home. For reasons we are not told, she had urgent and apparently large financial obligations. Her personal grief had to take a back seat. Survival was crucial.

She didn't have time to think about working her way through the proverbial "Ten Stages of Grief." She had to accept her situation immediately and do what she could.

The context implies that she had exhausted every normal means of payment. Apparently, she had already sold all her furniture and possessions. Nothing was left in the house. Her creditors threatened to take her children away and make them slaves.

She decided on what today might be called "Christian counseling." She went to Elisha the prophet for counsel.

"What shall I do for you?" he asked.

Wasn't it obvious? Perhaps he wanted her to verbalize her predicament so he could show her how only God could solve it.

Notice what he *didn't* do for her: He didn't loan her money, pay her debt, speak to her creditors about canceling the debt or even get them to extend the terms. He didn't work out an easy payment plan for her, recommend her for a job or offer to hide her children so her creditors wouldn't find them.

He led her to take the next step. "Tell me, what *do* you have in the house?" He pointed her *to her own reserves*, meager though they were. She replied that she had nothing with which to meet her personal needs, family needs and nothing to meet her public needs—the debt she owed.

"Your servant has nothing there at all *except* a little oil." Yes, she did have *something*.

Elisha instructed her to borrow empty vessels from her neighbors. No, not to borrow money or food. He told her to *collect her "emptinesses,"* as it were. "Not a few," but as many as she could gather. He instructed her to involve her family in the project.

Then he told her to bring them inside and shut the door. This was not meant to be a spectacular demonstration or public miracle, but done "in the secret place" to privately show God's mercy and grace to the widow. It is in the secret place that *we* abide under the shadow of the Almighty, and He can work on our behalf. (Psalm 91)

Then the miracle began to happen. All the "emptinesses" the widow lined up began to *fill with oil*, more than enough to sell for profit and pay her debts. She did business with God's provision. Beyond that, the oil was so abundant that all her future personal and family needs were supplied. "You can live on what is left," he said.

As the widow of a man who feared the Lord, I, too, am left with many "emptinesses." I can list them. I can line them up. But I must do my part and obey the Lord. No questions, no arguments, no trying to figure things out logically by myself.

I must bring *all* my "emptinesses" to God, and He will fill them *all*. Nevertheless, I must actively participate in His personal miracle on my behalf.

My little jar of oil, *whatever it is,* will be different from another widow's. My personal resource, the "nothing except . . ." in my house, may seem like a trifle, but that's when God's abundance and generosity takes over.

I have the Lord and all His provision. I have His oil, the oil that symbolizes the Holy Spirit in all His attributes and power. That oil can fill all my emptiness.

The Holy Spirit was with me even when I thought I had nothing "in my house." He had not left me when Ted left for heaven. The Lord promised, "My grace is sufficient for you." Therefore, "I can do all things through Christ who strengthens me." And, "My God shall supply all your need through His riches in Christ Jesus." Jesus invites me to ask Him so that I can receive His abundance!

The Lord has never failed anyone. If He fails you, you will be the first. He has never failed me, and surely He will not fail me now!

The Bible records other stories about widows. On another occasion, the widow of Zarephath in 1 Kings 17:9-16 gave the prophet the last of what she had. She was so destitute that she was gathering sticks for a fire to bake a cake (not the Pillsbury chocolate layer cake kind, but a simple biscuit-like Eastern pancake).

She had only a handful of flour and a little oil, not even a jar of oil like the widow in the previous story. She planned to make a final meal, and then she and her son expected to die of starvation.

The prophet asked her to make a cake for him *first*. How illogical and presumptuous that sounded! Nevertheless, she didn't ask any questions and acted by faith. Her obedience resulted in abundance! She and her son had plenty to eat. She never ran out of flour or oil!

The Lord performed a different kind of miracle for her than for the other widow. He gave the previous widow all of her supply *at one time*. He gave the widow of Zarephath hers *on a daily basis*, little by little as she needed it to fulfill her continuing need. Neither does the Lord expect unreasonable things from us. He meets us on the level of our ordinary resources.

The prophet didn't ask the widow for a steak or a tuna casserole. He asked her to be obedient according to her realistic resources.

God expresses a special care for widows! However, He requires that we prove Him and His supply by putting Him *first* above what we perceive are our own needs. If I seek *first* the Kingdom of God and His righteousness, He will meet all my needs, including daily necessities. (Matthew 6:25-34) More often it will be on a gradual, daily basis rather than all at once.

What is our priority need as singled out women?

Your goal as a widowed person is toward wholeness, toward a complete and satisfying lifestyle. It is not becoming numb to your pain and settling for what you have left. The price of wholeness is courage. The price is not too high, however, if you want happiness. It can be found in spite of any emptiness you feel now. [3]

God has many creative ways to care for us. He may do for us as He did for the people of Israel who journeyed in the desert for 40 long years. Their clothes and shoes *never wore out.* (Deuteronomy 29:5) Chapter eight, verse four adds that their feet did not swell! The Lord may sustain us *with what we already have* by keeping things in useable condition. (Even my body parts, Lord?)

I need to think about what God's provision means in my life, don't you? What do you and I have "in our houses" that relates to God's assignment for us? He is sufficient for every one of our "emptinesses."

Prudent planning

Jeremiah 29:11-14 has become precious to me:

'For I know the plans that I have for you,' declares the Lord, 'plans for welfare and not for calamity to give you a future and a hope. Then you will call upon Me and come and pray to Me, and I will listen to you. And you will seek Me and find Me, when you search for Me with all

your heart. And I will be found by you,' declares
the Lord.'

The Lord has thoughtfully prepared *good* plans
for us. He promises to take care of us *all* the days of our
lives. However, under His guidance we must also plan
wisely for ourselves. In 1900 a woman's life span was
about 50 years and a man's 48. The surviving widow
didn't expect to live alone for an extended time.

Now life expectancy for a man is about 70 and for
a woman about 78. In 1988 there were 12 million widows
in the United States, and it is expected there will be more
than 15 million within the current decade. The average
age of a widow today is about 56, which may give her 22
or more years as a widow.

The poet writes sentimentally, "Grow old
along *with me*—the best is yet to be."
Maybe—maybe not. Most women will
probably survive their mates and grow
old *alone.*

"Thus says the Lord: Set your house in order, for
you shall die and not live." That is repeated in Isaiah 38:1
and 2 Kings 20:1. Since death is inevitable, we singled
out women should be eager to redeem our remaining
days. When our spouses died, some of us were left with
many loose ends and practical things unsettled. Some
husbands don't even have a Last Will. If so, part of our
assignment may be to responsibly take care of practical
things, straighten them out and organize them. As a
single woman now, I am the only one responsible for my

house, my life, possessions and time. That includes not only financial affairs but family matters, relationships and areas of Christian witness. Each of us is different and needs the Lord's specific help to set her house in order. He expects us to be good stewards.

I can't retrace my steps and talk about death more wisely with my husband. Nevertheless, I can openly discuss my death and arrangements pertaining to my affairs with my family before I become ill, aged, or am otherwise unable to communicate.

Another part of my assignment as a Christian single is to share my Christian faith and my assurance of heaven lovingly and clearly with my family. I need to be concerned about *my* survivors too, those I love who will remain to go through the process of grief and adjustment without me.

Our husbands may have faithfully taken care of all such matters. However, that is not always the case. If they were too busy or reticent about such necessary discussions, it's part of our assignment to do so while we're living.

Evaluate the advice of others

Other people aren't walking in your shoes. They don't know what size or style you wear, or the problem you may have with your crooked big toe! Your shoes must fit. When God gives you your assignment, it will fit perfectly.

Simply collecting the opinions of others as to your probable assignment can be hazardous to your emotional and spiritual health.

It might cloud your decision-making process. Everyone seems to be an expert when it comes to knowing what *you* should do with your life. They offer well-meaning advice on where you should live, whether you should live alone or with someone, whether you should get a job, whether you should marry again and what they think your assignment should be.

However, let's be careful of subtle pride that might imply, "Don't give me any advice. I know better."

We should thank people for counsel they give us whether we asked for it or not, and ask them to continue praying for us. We do well to seek counsel from mature Christians, a pastor, close friends, our family and professional counselors as needed. "Without consultation, plans are frustrated. But with many counselors they succeed" (Proverbs 15:22). God does use people and circumstances to lead us, but ultimately we must look to the Lord alone for our assignment.

When you begin to understand what your assignment might be, even good friends may not understand your reasoning and perhaps not agree with your conclusion. Nevertheless, you are responsible to God, your Maker, who is now your Husband. He will see you through to fulfill the assignment He gives you.

Don't just sit there

The blind beggar Bartimaeus was sitting by the roadside having a personal pity party. When Jesus came by, he shouted (according to the Modern Language version) "Take pity on me!" Pity was all he asked Jesus for.

The disciples brought a message from Jesus to Bartimaeus. "Take courage; get up, He is calling you" (Mark 10:49 Amplified).

Here I am, a widow, sitting by the roadside of life. Jesus calls *me* to get up and *asks me* what I want. Is *pity* really all I want from Jesus and from others? Or simply *comfort?* If so, I'm not asking largely enough. Pity is not what Jesus wants to give me. Comfort is only the fringe benefit of great things He wants to give me.

Amy Carmichael comments, "He calleth thee *by name.* He calleth thee *to new service,* and for that service He will give new vision and new power to follow Jesus in the way."

Jesus encouraged Bartimaeus to ask specifically and receive largely. He got his blind eyes opened—far more than he initially requested. Pity wouldn't have helped him much. After Jesus healed him, he no longer needed the pity that he thought was his all-consuming need.

I receive what I ask for. So I'm asking for God's assignment and counting on His abundant provision to accomplish it through me. Aren't you?

A new mountain to climb?

The Bible says that Caleb "wholly followed the Lord" in his youth and was still doing so in old age. In Joshua chapter 14 we read that he *patiently waited 45 years* from the beginning of his vision and direction from the Lord (his assignment) before he was able to get on with it. By that time he was *already advanced in age.*

Do I use the excuse that it is obviously too late for me to fulfill anything the Lord laid on my heart in my early years? I may see only a mountain of limitations ahead of me. Nevertheless, the Lord doesn't put mountains in my path to stop or block me. I can ask, as Caleb did, "Give me this mountain!" What mountain? Whatever mountain (assignment) the Lord sets before me, including my immediate mountain of singleness again.

Our mountain might be new territory to conquer, to make productive, to stand on top of and view still more new horizons. What could those new horizons be in my life? What vision, direction or assignment did the Lord show me perhaps earlier in my life? Although I may not have been able to fulfill it while I was married and raising a family, *now I am free to do so!*

My age doesn't matter—Caleb was 85
when he negotiated for a new mountain
to conquer. What excuse do *I* have?

I'm praying over a list of "things I would like to do." Enjoyable things—dreams, desires, visions. If I truly delight in the Lord, He promises to give me the desires of my heart. (Psalm 20:4) In an amazing and sometimes unexpected way, *the desires of my heart* turn out to be *God's desires for me!* In our new role as singled out women, we have permission to dream again and to follow God's dreams for us. He will give us the courage.

Dream again

Lord, daring to dream again
sounds so good,
but sometimes
memories of broken dreams
haunt me.
Help me to let go of the pain

that keeps me from responding
to Your gentle nudging.
Your presence encourages me
to set fear aside
and to become
a spiritual risk-taker.
I want *Your* dreams for me
to be *my* dreams as well.[4]

Let us pick up our laid-aside dreams like a bow long unused and shoot some arrows to the future. However, we must aim at *specific* targets. If we aim at nothing, we are sure to hit nothing! God provides the target—His assignment—and gives us archery equipment and instruction.

Please excuse me?

For us singled out women who have been serving the Lord with our husbands, now is not the time to retreat and cease our ministry. Do we back off and do less and less because we are "only widows" now, and people can't expect us to shoulder much ministry?

Paul has a strong command for us in 1 Thessalonians 4:1, "We instructed you *how to live in order to please God,* as in fact you *are* living. Now we ask you and urge you in the Lord Jesus *to do this more and more.*"

Have *I* been excusing myself from some ministry opportunities because of my new status as a widow? The best "balm of Gilead" for my own loss is to reach out to others who are in need. A singled out friend wrote me:

Since my husband's passing four years
ago, I have found great blessing in touching

others with encouragement. God gives so much back to me! I'm praying that your time of grieving will not be prolonged, but will be a stepping stone to greater paths of service and endeavor as He leads.

Then she shared Isaiah 58:10,11 as marching orders with promise:

And if you give yourself to the hungry, and satisfy the desire of the afflicted, then your light will rise in darkness, and your gloom will become like midday.
And the Lord will continually guide you, and satisfy your desires in scorched places, and give strength to your bones; And you will be like a watered garden, and like a spring of water whose waters do not fail.

Jesus said that if we try to save and preserve our lives, we will lose them. It is a downhill slide. However, if we lose our lives, that is, *spend ourselves for others,* we will find abundant life and personal fulfillment. The bonus? The Lord will generously satisfy *our needs,* if we invest ourselves in the needs of others.

Since we suffered a human loss, we may feel as though we are walking in the darkness of night. The Lord promised in the above passage to change our night of gloom into the brightness of noonday. *Light* is a necessity for health and well-being and an antidote to mental depression.

God will strengthen my bones? Oh, how I need that! My loss has given me emotional arthritis. I feel bowed down and even physically achy. I need the Lord's "hot springs" treatment.

The Lord will make us like spring-fed, well-watered gardens! What a promise for us in our dry, sun-scorched, desert condition! Let's claim that promise as we accept our assignment from the Lord as *His singled out, chosen handmaidens!*

End

(But really a beginning for you!)

End Notes

Chapter 1: Singled out by God

1 Elliot, Elisabeth, *Loneliness,* (Nashville: Thomas Nelson Publishers, 1988), pp.35-37, 40.

2 Choy, Leona, "Not Alone" *Life-Stop Crowding Me!* (Paradise:Ambassadors For Christ, Inc., 1992) p. 10.

3 Aldrich, Sandra, *Living Through the Loss of Someone You Love,* (Ventura, Regal Books, 1990), p. 189.

4 *Grief Steps I,* (Pittsburgh: Publication of the THEOS Foundation, Inc. "Survivors' Outreach" series, undated) p. 2.

Chapter 2: Experiencing Good Grief

1 Lutzer, Erwin W., *Coming to Grips With Death and Dying,* (Chicago: Moody Press, 1992), p. 32.

2 "Linkage Between Love and Grief," *Chera Fellowship Publication,* Vol. 2, #2, I.F.C.A., Grandville, MI. p. 9.

3 Manning, Doug, *Don't Take My Grief Away: What to Do When You Lose a Loved One,* (New York: Harper & Row, Publishers Inc. 1984), pp. 63,64.

4 Ibid. p. 64,65.

5 Adapted by Anita Speer Smith, *Grief Steps I,* ibid, p. 15.

Chapter 3: Don't Push Me Through the "Stage" door!

1 Grief Sounds, *Grief Sounds I,* (Pittsburgh: Publication of the THEOS Foundation, Inc. Echoes of the Journey Through Grief series, undated) p. 2.

2 Elliot, Elisabeth, *A Path Through Suffering: Discovering the Relationship Between God's Mercy and Our Pain,* (Ann Arbor, Servant Publications, 1990), p. 164.

3 *Regret and Guilt,* Grief Sounds I, ibid, p. 16.

4 Woodson, Meg, *The Toughest Days of Grief* (Grand Rapids:

Zondervan Publishing House, 1994), pp. 98, 100.

5 Bayly, Joseph, *The Last Thing We Talk About: Help and Hope for Those Who Grieve*, (Elgin: David C. Cook, 1969), pp. 46-48.

6 Dycus, Barbara, *God's Design for Broken Lives*, (Springfield: Gospel Publishing House, 1994), p. 115.

7 Woods, Deborah, From Sundown to Sun Up, *Grief Steps I*, ibid, p. 15.5 Choy,

8 Choy, Leona, "Morning," unpublished poem, 1995.

Chapter 4: Making It Through Those "Firsts"

1 Choy, Leona, "Storm" *Heaven and Nature Sing*, (Paradise: Ambassadors For Christ, Inc. 1994), p.37.

2 Choy, Leona, "Letter From Glory," unpublished poem, 1992.

3 Choy, Leona, "Falling Leaf," unpublished poem, 1993.

Chapter 5: Checking My Scriptural Anchors

1 Yancey, Philip, *Where is God When It Hurts?* (Grand Rapids: Zondervan Publishing House, 1977) pp. 179,180.

2 Stanley, Charles, *How to Handle Adversity,* (Nashville: Oliver-Nelson Books, Thomas Nelson Publishers 1989) pp. 17,18.

3 Peterson, James and Warrick, Pamela, *On Being Alone*, Guide For Widowed Persons, (Washington: AARP Publications, 1988) p.7.

4. Lutzer, ibid. p. 38.

Chapter 6: Refocusing My Relationships

1 Source untraceable.

2 Cushenbery, Donald C. and Cushenbery, Rita Crossley *Coping with Life After Your Mate Dies*, (Grand Rapids: Baker Book House, 1991), pp. 67, 70, 79.

3 The Search for Meaning, *Grief Sounds I,* p. 8.

Chapter 7: Potholes on Adjustment Avenue

1 Swindoll, Chuck, *For Those Who Hurt*, (Portland: Multnomah Press, 1977)

2 Elliot, Elisabeth, *Facing the Death of Someone You Love*, (Westchester: Good News Publishers, 1973), p. 8.

3 Mumford, Amy Ross, *It Hurts to Lose a Special Person*, (Elgin:Accent Books, David C. Cook Publishing Co., 1982.

4 Sanders, J. Oswald, *Facing Loneliness: The Starting Point of a New Journey*, (Grand Rapids: Discovery House, 1988) p. 8.

5 Choy, Leona, "Always," *Life—Stop Crowding Me!*, (Paradise: Ambassadors For Christ, Inc. 1992), p.189.

6 Source untraceable.

7 Choy, Leona, "Silence", *Songs of My Pilgrimage*, (Paradise: Ambassadors For Christ, Inc. 1994), p. 39.

Chapter 8: Resetting My Compass

1 Mumford, ibid. (pages are not numbered)

2 Source untraceable.

3 Choy, Leona, "My Portion," *Songs of My Pilgrimage*, (Paradise: Ambassadors For Christ, Inc. 1994), p. 3.

4 Lawrenz, Mel and Green, Daniel, *Life After Grief: How to Survive Loss and Trauma*, (Grand Rapids: Baker Books, 1995), pp. 119, 120.

5 Dycus, Barbara, *God's Design for Broken Lives*, (Springfield: Gospel Publishing House, 1994), p. 113.

Chapter 9: Receiving God's Assignment

1 Romey, Beverly, A Survivor, *Grief Steps I*, ibid, p. 8

2 Swindoll, Chuck, *For Those Who Hurt*, (Portland: Multnomah Press, 1977)

3 Woods, Deborah, *Who Am I? And Where Am I Going?*, Grief Steps II, ibid, p. 13.

4 Author unknown